Planet on Strike

John Pairman Brown

PLANET
ON
STRIKE

THE SEABURY PRESS · NEW YORK

Copyright © 1970 by John Pairman Brown
Library of Congress Catalog Card Number: 78-100351
Design by Carol Basen
666-1269-C-5
Printed in the United States of America

For
George, Felicity, Maryam, and David

261.

Preface

This book was written by a middle-aged person for the young, who are likely not to read it, but with whom he still works. Not as objects of paternal or missionary concern, but as comrades in a risky forced push into the future, in spite of our differences in hairdo and domestic arrangements. Another middle-aged person looking over our shoulders may feel I reach conservative conclusions by revolutionary logic. Well, the aim is helping stabilize a global community to carry out fundamental changes demanded by the needs of the planet, of the poor, of our hearts, and laid on us by an old book in all our hands.

I have here to present more than conventional thanks to The Seabury Press for buying a pig in a poke; and a more than conventional disclaimer that it doesn't necessarily express the views of any incorporated body—not even the Free Church of Berkeley, whose trustees released me from what seemed like more urgent jobs to write it. It does express, as best I could, the conclusions required by *The Liberated Zone*—the suggestions for personal life which the Church Divinity School of the Pacific kindly repatriated me from the Middle East to make. Once again Dick York and my wife, Emily, held my hand when the work went badly.

My diligent editor across the continent, and the slothful editor in my heart, still point to faults of matter and organization. I can only explain that the world's laser-beam never gave me a chance to cool down. Each morning brought new reports of daring and folly: footsteps in lunar dust, poisons in the seabed. Each night I went to sleep with the sound in my ears of that bombing which has brought on a planetary revolt. But also, just during the writing I've felt the growth of a precious community, seen and unseen, whose views I was simply recording. On our bootleg Telstar channel, in spite of war, pollution, and resentment, there is going out a message of hope.

JOHN PAIRMAN BROWN

Berkeley, California
August 12, 1969
Anniversary of William Blake's death, 1827.

Contents

Introduction:
The Revolution
and Its Demands

Unlicensed by any authorities, a global underground communications network has sprung up,
calling for a planetary strike. It's responding to a crisis
of violence on three levels: against natural order, social
order, individual freedom. More often than not, the
strikers meet violence with counter-violence. To that extent, there's no revolution happening, but only a change
of masters—which may help things some, but in the end
not enough. The trouble is, the demands presented haven't
been thought through, they're merely tactical. But if they
could find their proper anchorage in the past, they'd become our bellbuoys in the fog blowing landward from the
sea of the future.

So on the vacant lots of the old society, in between
skirmish and counter-skirmish of police and militants, I
remove the litter to uncover three hopeful new shoots,
springing from layers of the present which were deposited
by successive periods of evolution. Corresponding to our
roots in the biological environment, our extension in soci-

ety, and our transcendence of both in individual freedom, we discover an authentic triple revolution of life: the *green* revolution of conservation, the *peace* revolution of liberated community, the *inner* revolution of integrity. The first part of this book outlines the shape they're beginning to take on.

Through the imperfect strategy of the strike, men and women around the globe today are claiming an actual role in that revolution, for the first time daring to become themselves. *The human race has issued a non-negotiable demand for life.* The second part of this book analyzes the renewal in the periods of our individual life required by the novel situation. We've inherited symbolic forms to shape each life-phase. In face of the urgent revolutions for conservation and peace, these forms must be radically adapted to build up a new level of personal consistency— the inner revolution. As soon as we start to work out those adaptations, we see they were precisely what time's arrow (which also generated the crisis of violence) had all along intended.

"On Strike, Shut It Down"

The cracked leather of traditional institutions has a flexible new wineskin inside; the rising ferment of people's rebellion is the actual sap which must be poured into it. The young bear the future; revolution wins out in the end. Both young and old have a hand in determining whether the revolution is violent or not; unilateral concessions are required of both sides. To avoid further bloodshed and stiffening of positions, the old must relinquish the power which in any case will be taken from them by death. To avoid haphazard rebuilding, the young must voluntarily accept and refine old institutions, which in some form will be forced on them by the need to run society.

The old are older today, and comparatively there are fewer of them. As technology accelerates the pace of historic time, the decade when their opinions were formed constantly recedes further from the present. Until population increase is damped, the majority will be under thirty. The old men in the managerial classes of the planet, whether corporate or socialist, were raised on humorless self-denying ideologies of economics, which further distorted the one-sided insights of Calvin and Marx. The great thing was to work hard, plow one's labor back into the system (the Economy or Party), and by its gratitude assure a stable niche for one's children. Today both means and ends are dropping away.

The peoples that used to supply raw materials and cheap labor to the Great Powers are asking for them back again. The lower middle class is less and less interested in providing the clerical help to run the System. As the System automates, it faces a generation which rejects the role of knowledgeable consumer. Women and children picket the expensive missile systems their menfolk set up to protect them. Prague doesn't wish to be saved from capitalist intervention. The sons of Defense Secretaries occupy Harvard buildings. Meanwhile judges, bishops, politicians go on speaking as if old sanctions were still operative. Young people are thrown back on their own perceptions, crudely formed by the mass media—but not so crudely as to miss the contrast between professed and actual goals.

The old men, who can't read the signals, in frustration tighten traditional controls. As the helicopters of nightmare drift from cradle to cradle, in Saigon, in Bolivia, in Tokyo, in Berkeley, mothers and children and old people, seeing themselves crop-dusted like insects with toxic agents, in rage and hope strike out against bullying. The spontaneous agreement of Catholics around the world to shelve the encyclical *Humanae Vitae* shows a confidence they know what's good for their families, their society, their environment. Liberation movements, defeating eight-engine bombers with bicycles, tanks with molotov cocktails, bayonets with flowers, are a political affirmation of the dignity of man—which their American and Russian masters once meant to affirm by *their* revolutions. At the fragile point of society, where young people are computer-dated with jobs, there's a massive refusal to accept what they can only see as paternalism and complicity. *The planet is on strike.*

It's hard for a ruling class to be reminded that its status rests on the destruction of private property in a Boston Tea Party. Daughters of the American Revolution still must try to see that the liberated young woman taking a daily pill is intending to carry on *their* work. The University is embarrassed at its origin in the protest of a Socrates against illegitimate claims, when the underprivileged ask for it to be turned over to them once again. At the mythical fountainhead of that Judaeo-Christian heritage invoked by commencement speakers lie the non-negotiable demands of a brick-makers' union. Around the globe goes up a shout, "On strike, shut it down."

The rebels, with all their shortcomings, have still caught the masters at the weak point of their rhetoric. Establishment anger towards blacks, students, Viet Cong, hippies is frustration at being inhibited by its own principles from wiping them out on the spot. It should indeed be shocking to see guns carried into college administration buildings—but hardly for a public bored with seeing guns fired into peasant villages. There must be a better way than guns; but few persons in America (or Russia) have illustrated it, and few of *them* have had medals struck in their lifetime. Perhaps the strikers fail to make the best case, concentrating on superficial grievances or amnesty for themselves; all the more reason to help them find it.

For the case is there. The voices of protest, however shrill, inconsistent, parochial, each are getting at some injustice or folly which cries out for instant correction. Even though every set of infuriating non-negotiable demands should prove improper, the principle of non-negotiable demands corresponds to the way things actually are. Our right to exist on this planet, although not our own invention, isn't something we must wheedle from any big daddy as we bring him his slippers. The unalterable demands of the strikers aren't all that different from the "inalienable rights" of life, liberty, and the pursuit of happiness; or from something we may still remember, the thirst for God's justice and vindication which admits no substitute.

The planetary environment, pushed beyond its breaking point, is also going on strike: Lake Erie is dead, the butterflies are disappearing, industrial air is unbreathable. The ecology has an unexpected ally, the young of the human species, whose diurnal cycle, violated by noise and office-routine, by distraction and boredom, by pills and pills, is refusing to function. Our technicians in research and development branches, in crowd-control seminars, screened for psychological stability, could keep all else in line, but not their own kids. Mrs. Leigh Roycroft at seventeen wrote the *San Francisco Chronicle* (April 16, 1969): "When I was four years old we lived on Nellis Air Force Base in Las Vegas. I remember so clearly, too clearly, the misty early mornings when sleep was still half claiming. I remember my mother coming to wake my brother and me on the occasion of still another in-atmosphere nuclear test. I can still see with nightmare clarity that mushroom cloud rising and expanding, tinted rose and orange and all the colors of life as the sun came up over the desert. O great silent majority, did you ever have the bomb before your breakfast? I went, for a short while, to school in Fairfield, home of Travis Air Force Base. My school faced hills on which stood the gaunt gantrys of missiles planted during the Cuban crisis. It went so well with my white-washed American history."

The American homeowner and the Asiatic insurgent are stuck with each other in this telluric closed system, a potential Eden walled off by the cherubim of galactic space. Why is it so hard for them to get together on it? Mutual insecurity cuts deep. It's well not to underestimate the hostility of Israelis and Arabs, Turks and Armenians, Malaysians and Chinese. Hardest of all to placate are those responsible for mass death; they're threatened with total collapse if they should admit their guilt. How can the murderer be brought back into decent society? To avoid despairing of people, we must find a way to say that the enemy isn't evil people but evil powers—and then deal with them. The fact of broken orders calls for a different answer than preventive detention of militants on the one hand, and glacially gradual reform of institutions on the other. The gap is widening too fast for any such putty to fill it.

The idiocy of two missile-systems facing each other across the Arctic underlines a monstrous psychological fact: distrust. No narrower is the rift between uptight parent and dropout child: anger, silence, refusal to credit the other with wishing to bridge it. And who will reconcile the robin on the lawn with the DDT manufacturer?

Any spontaneous response is quickly overlaid with time, habit. We mentally block out jails, war; out of sight, out of mind. We jump at the chance to authenticate the lies told about us; as well be hung for a sheep as a lamb. No abstract goodwill overcomes distrust; required are work, suffering, discipline. But when our antagonisms push both sides into unrepairable damage to society or the planet, we see that trust is necessary. Then it must be possible. Like other living things, it's only born of its own kind. That orange only ripens on a tree whose sap flows back and back to a root outside space and time. Like other trees, its growth is often stunted; but it doesn't have to be, it can fill the world.

The Breaking and Renewal of Natural Orders

As all the systems of global biology and society interlock, as all human beings intersect, the massive job of renewal can't be broken up into absolutely separate components; it's a single cake. Still, a cake elaborate enough for a fresh start, a birthday or wedding, has to be built up in layers, and then cut in sectors. The two parts of this book slice renewal in those two ways at right angles to each other, beginning with the three layers of natural order.

Planetary evolution generated in turn two levels of organization: nature and society. A man or woman—a biological organism caught up in a stream of history—is the place they overlap. The individual appears to be the sum of his biological inheritance and of his contacts with other individuals. But that sum stands on a higher third level: the freedom of a being aware of having emerged from earlier phases of evolution.

We're the top growth of the tree of life, spreading upwards to meet the sun above the lower canopies of biology and history. But the world-tree has been attacked on our level by an undiagnosed blight, which spreads back down from us. Again and again its golden apples crumble into the cindery fruits of Sodom. Our intelligence lets us evade, for a time, the limits placed by fixed global resources on the spread of every other species. But that spore of reason has puffed up into the toadstools of overpopulation and technology, which overload the environment with unsuitable items. Right from the beginning, social order has been only a dream; history is the record of class struggle, oppression of subject populations.

Only in our own years have all three levels of violence been seen as interrelated and of equal urgency. While each was always latent, those which depend on developed technology both appear later, and are harder to reverse. Although the disruption of global ecology came last, it will take a global effort to undo it.

The agency responsible for destruction of natural orders obviously includes ourselves. Still, even the person most directly responsible for the damage—the racist, general, broker, logger, bully, advertiser, cardinal—can find plausible excuses; he's operating inside a system not of his own making. It's true also that at some point he made a decision not to fight it.

As corruption builds up, the claims of evil become more insistent, but at the same time more strongly contrasted with our instincts. Individuals through their immersion in an exploitative system either consciously assent to violence, or actively initiate it. But they also suffer it directly from others, and indirectly from the environment. *Every person is both victim and accomplice in the breaking of orders.*

The same intelligence and freedom involved in the breaking also makes restoration of the orders possible. It would be hopeless to try and begin reconstruction from the ground up in any one generation. But, just as the dark thread of violence can be traced indefinitely far back, so can a golden thread of renewal—the history of hope. By it we lay hold on the green revolution, replacing economic "development" of the planet by ecological decontamination, recycling all materials. In the peace revolution we replace individual aggression by persuasion within community. The inner revolution means replacing self-assertion with gentleness. We can summarize the triple breakthrough in the old hope of a new Jerusalem: at once a restored garden, with its river and tree of life; a city at peace; a building whose stones are the pearls of individual lives. A new planet, new community, new humanity.

Our New Fidelity

Last Maundy Thursday when my wife and I went to our Free Church, a boy with an Indian headband far out on some trip came up and asked if we were Quakers. The word has gone out that one class of persons anyway, through consistency over the centuries, has merited trust. Kind reader, is he called by your name? If not, now would be a good time for reappraisal of self.

For we do hold our life in our hands. Each revolution, even when it ends up in new slavery, is still affirming the springtime of individual liberation. The new planetary citizen, a Hammarskjöld, goes directly where the threat to community is greatest; and that's only the negative side of a new fidelity starting to breed true. Under the most hopeful assumptions, it will take a number of generations to be fairly sure that the threat has been averted. What level of spirituality will be built up by men of all cultures actually cooperating over those centuries?

The individual man or woman is given the best chance of working into renewal at the turning-points of life which begin a new phase of its trajectory. Some are unique: birth, puberty, death. Some are periodic: falling casualty, celebration. Some may be either: entering into sexual fulfilment, taking on vocation. Each stage rests on a biological function essential to maintain either the individual or the species. Each also generates a social grouping: the family, working team, class, school, the State. The biological and social functions of each stage stand for some aspect of individual freedom which goes beyond them. People become most aware of violence and renewal, both in nature and society, at those interchanges.

Personal renewal into integrity can only be effected through a symbolism of word, action, or object, operating at the roots of nature and history. The scene of that happening is community—what in some sense we may call the

Church. Through community, individuals have their best leverage on politics to push forward the green revolution, and in part the peace revolution; but on a longer view, the community itself is the spreading area of peace.

In the history of community, the torch we inherit and pass on, the claim is made that the inner revolution has already in principle been carried out. Individual crises are given universal meaning by their anchorage in an historical event so distant (and even in its own time long expected) that all peoples can today recognize in it a fountainhead of their own history. Our new awareness of violence and renewal makes us look at the origins of the Church in the life of Jesus under a different light. The current revolution requires us to reinterpret the ancient revolution of which he was the center. This reinterpretation won't be arbitrary. For he represents the coming-of-age of Western history, which in turn plays the key role in planetary history. The violence against which he struggled, and his new definition of community, are the sources of current breakage and current fidelity.

The wise men we still fall back on, both in West and East, describe our fulfilment as taking the right course— varying with the local development of land transport, a path or road; the Way. Seafaring societies envisage it as a voyage by water. And it not merely has to fit the unique parabola of our personal development; the future terrain we must build it across hasn't even been deposited yet by the volcanic or sedimentary processes of the present— namely, the sum of all our individual routes. No television into time will show us that driver, the future Me, or the deteriorating vehicle of his body. The one sign we can be sure of finding is ROAD UNDER CONSTRUCTION.

As monitor of the march, many have followed Dante the Florentine out of the dark waste to see the stars. Others stand with Bunyan the tinker, a load on their back and a book in their hand, looking up to the distant wicket gate: "What must I do to be saved?" Some children I know have set up a permanent picket line against a certain Lord of the Dark Tower. Russians have Zhivago, Vietnamese their much-suffering sister Kieu. But beyond poetry, allegory, fairy tale, fiction, epic, we also need as plain a map as may be of the unfinished road. So I've undertaken here, writing not far from the Hayward fault and under a target moon, to draw up a simplified guide to the overnight lodgings we'll all be staying at, Americans and others alike, on our journey under protest across the landscape of revolution.

part I: The Phases
of Revolution

chapter ONE

Green Revolution: Renewal of the Environment

Throughout the universe, higher levels of organization imitate lower levels—and always with important novelties. Things have more detail, both in space and time, than myth or speculation ever guessed. Not surprising; since our myth-making faculty is just one feature of cosmic self-understanding. We can be sure also that the universe is more complicated than our minds, however scientific, have yet perceived. Still we must act on what they report to date.

The Patterns of Natural Order

The physical world repeats patterns on very different scales in space, and thus sets a precedent for biology and history in time. The *atom* has a nucleus of heavy particles with a hiveful of electrons buzzing around it. In most of the universe, atoms are bound by shared electrons into simple *molecules*, which are then built in extremely large numbers into the regular patterns of gas, liquid, crystal. As nuclear forces fade out and electric forces cancel, a new type of force becomes discernible, the gravitational. By it *solar systems* are held together, patterned like the atom, but simpler and less regular. As nuclear and electric forces limit the size of a nucleus, gravity and thermodynamics limit the size of a star. Up to ten billion stars, thinly dispersed as a gas, form rotating *galaxies*. They in turn, up to about a trillion, dispersed at random fill what looks like a finite expanding *space*. Its size is somehow determined by the "surface" tension of the matter it bears, curved in on itself like a soap-bubble in one more dimension.

Again, the several dozen fugitive particles of nuclear decay may be pointing to a lower level of organization, so that each proton or electron would in turn be a structured little world. And our "universe" might conceivably be built along some dimension with others like itself into a bigger arrangement. Pascal suggests that the array of structures both below the atom and beyond the galaxy is repeated forever, so that the universe would be doubly infinite; each flea would bite a big flea, and have a little flea biting him.

The known universe is a product of time, probably by expansion during ten billion years from an original tight beginning. But although the building-blocks, from elementary particles to galaxies, are subject to change, they persist over long periods comparable to the age of the whole. This state of affairs is greatly modified in special environments like our planet, bathed in a constant flow of radiation from a sun-star. The energy of that stream builds atoms into organizations far more complex than anything else we know in the cosmos, with properties not suggested by the physicist's world—life, consciousness, love. We are the center; Ptolemy was right and Copernicus was wrong. The continuity of protoplasm behind us, back to the original condensation of the sea, is itself a fact of cosmic age; for it's occupied a large portion (perhaps twenty percent) of the assumed total age of the universe, during which many supernovas have been born and died.

Planetary evolution differs in important ways from cosmic.

Elaboration through time. Galaxies and stars may not be much younger than atoms and protons; physical patterns could have crystallized on all levels at nearly the same time. But on the planet, structures were elaborated in time, from the protein-rich original sea to proto-viruses, one-celled organisms, complex organisms, vertebrates, land animals, more-or-less rational man. The spherical shell of life we inhabit has fewer atoms than the planet's iron heart, its crystalline layers, or the first sea; but it's not repetitive like a crystal or liquid, it has unending variety, functional specialization. And in its hierarchy of order, each higher center of organization is more recent than the one below it.

Acceleration of evolutionary time. Evolutionary time, as measured by the appearance of new levels of order against standard physical time, has speeded up a billion-fold. The Palaeolithic period is comparable to ages of biological evolution; and it's true that the mutations of flu virus happen in the historic periods of years—perhaps triggered by social and medical change. But over against cosmic and planetary evolution, our decades represent a new phenomenon, where features of the biological and social environment change drastically in ten earth-orbits around the sun.

Fragility of living structures. Physical structures are too big or too widespread to be affected by man's intelligence. We have nothing to split a star or planet with. Our splitting of nuclei repeats something which happens anyway in stars, its products have an advance slot in the system. On the planet, every level of organization is vulnerable to environmental changes—an eruption, earthquake, ice age, tropical age, increase in solar radiation, meteor-fall. Species or phyla fall prey to destructive mutations, to their neighbors. And the evolution has culminated in a system of organization—ourselves—with the power to destroy itself, lower levels, and large parts of the environment which has evolved along with them.

In spite of these big differences, planetary evolution maintains previous levels of organization and builds them into contemporary structures. A redwood's grain summarizes its push upwards and its bracing against gravity over a thousand years. The animals in a square mile of grassland are the result of hundreds of millions of years of development; their distribution holds the key to the making and breaking of land-bridges between the continents. The spices in our kitchens, a cross-section of global botany, summarize the whole history of commerce since the Roman Empire; the cassia of Solomon and Sappho originated in the Mekong Delta.

Long before modern science, understanding of our roots in ecology was available through myth or speculation. The nine months of gestation have always on some level been seen to echo the emergence of life from the sea. The feeling for sacred groves and the earth mother was reborn in the eighteenth century through identification with the wilderness, at the point of its destruction by industrialism. And in turn these biological patterns are taken up and transformed on the levels of society and individual freedom.

The Breaking of Biological Order

The physical properties of water determine where life can exist. As the fixing of the simplest charged particle, the proton, water parallels in the living environment the flux of charged particles in the sun. Also then it stands for all environmental orders, the reservoirs which supply the water of our life.

It seems a general rule that, whatever can happen, will happen; every potentiality in the end is realized. The fact that biology and society are vulnerable to technology and overpopulation implies that somewhere, sometime, the wound will actually be struck. But to the responsible conscious agent, that breaking of natural order is seen under the category of *wrong*. In the first age of literature which remains definitive for us, the poet shows how the inexplicable act would appear to a power underlying the space-time manifold: "My people have done two evils; they have rejected me, the fountain of living water, to dig for themselves reservoirs, broken reservoirs, which cannot hold water" (Jeremiah 2: 13). As the imagined environmental Golden Age is violated, all the orders fall away: biological order is altered by weeds, social order by murder, individual order by death newly seen as threat, "For you are dust, and to dust you will return."

In the past, only a rare observer could note irreversible changes in the environment, as when Plato records that great houses in Athens stood built with timber from hills where in his day only the bee pastured. Ours is the first generation universally aware of such changes—the introduction of chlorinated hydrocarbons as pesticides around the globe. Violence between groups has also taken new forms, to which the mass media create new awareness, both among executioners and victims.

The original biological rhythms of our life have been built by history as fixed-cycle components into systems undergoing ever more rapid change. At most, puberty is anticipated by two or three years, death postponed by twenty or thirty. No wonder then so many take on chemicals for metabolic adjustment to the altered environment. We that make do with traditional caffeine and alcohol seem the queer ones, who can't attune our ears to the amplifiers, our eyes to the cathode-ray tube, our hands to the freeway.

Americans, living in affluent communities, parasitic on other parts of the globe even for water, form an exaggerated picture of what technology can do. Inherited biological and historical structures are not indefinitely malleable like gold. No counter-technology will work against oil-slicks and deforestation; only the skill and restraint which conform so close to the contours of nature as to be a second nature.

As body rhythms point back to the beginning of life on the planet, our discomfort at violence points ahead to a planet again waste and void when demonism has run its course. The same old books which anticipated our discovery of evolution are still far in advance of us, in their concrete symbolism of the end of world illustrating where our road leads. If our politics is to steer a clumsy United Nations into the right way, it must be guided by delicate individual compasses. We enter deeper into ourselves, trace out each broken root in our earth mother, patiently set up conditions for new life. Our emotions, reason, consciousness—each aspect of our freedom—are somehow a blossoming from the basic conditions of the amoeba or the cell: assimilation and reproduction.

Biological Roots of Our Freedom

Assimilation. In tropical climates, the energy of primary human organization can go simply into assuring the food-supply. In colder climates, we feel like working harder—and must, to assure clothing and shelter also. Unusually favorable environments like Polynesia, with guaranteed food-supply, produce societies with built-in population controls, where the bulk of energy flows into an elaborate ingrown artistic culture. The original function of economic, political, social power is to put a protective frontier around foodlands or waters. Getting food, or its symbolic equivalent, is the primary need which pushes the male into his vocation. Money in young America is appropriately called "bread," as in Rome it was called "cows" (*pecunia*).

Our superabundance of energy can lend itself to misdirection, and therefore from time to time does. In a character where the emotions are diverted inward or downward, which Freud ingeniously called the anal fixation, money the food-equivalent is transformed into a dung-equivalent, as in the constipated miser, the stock figure of comedy.

In a simple society, community is manifested by sharing the food-supply which it exists to protect. The characteristic form of community is the feast. In the temperate climates of the West, the feast is celebrated with special vestments in a temple—the symbolic use of food, shelter, and clothing.

Primary aggressiveness aims at capturing the enemy's food-supply. Judging our neighbor's fears by our own, we credit him with preparing to anticipate an attack of our own on him. Our imagination of the worst is self-fulfilling, giving us a permanent motive of union for the self-defense which always spills over into pre-emptive strikes.

Reproduction. Sexuality and hunger compete for our attention, generating love and comradeship. In different ways for the man and the woman, sexuality is a detaching of something from the self as a beginning of new life. It too can become diverted like money, and get assimilated to the excretory organs it shares. Love is an intenser form of community; but the sexual act, except in the symbolic form of a dance, is less well adapted than the feast to public cult. Males of the human species, lacking (apart from their beards) ornamental secondary sexual characteristics, compensate by adorning the feast with music and dance.

Wherever social patterns disintegrate, sexuality like money-getting becomes an end in itself. The Greeks called interest on a loan *tokos*, "begetting." With us, sexuality is a dominant theme of the advertising that urges us to move out of anal fixation and spend money—the muck that's no use unless spread. Again, we have more children than is to the planet's interest, from fear that the enemy, imitating our aggression, will outnumber us: "Happy is the man who has his quiver full of them; he will not be ashamed when he speaks with his enemy in the gate." *Lebensraum* for all those kids is the secondary motive of aggression—which after a while, summing up money-getting and child-getting, becomes the final end in itself. Since the sexual motive is thought higher than the monetary, wars for economic expansion are motivated in heroic ages through the abduction of a frail Helen by some foreign Paris. In our unheroic age, the pretext for mass slaughter of civilians, with attendant prostitution, is the fiction of potent black or yellow men coming at our womenfolk with their military or sexual "tools."

As sexual and working energy wane, the world needs our death to make room for younger men and women. Besides the urge to beget a family and community, we have built into us a complementary acquiescence in death. When the death-wish gets out of hand, it takes the forms of self-hate, proneness to accidents, the courting of failure, suicide. If we can project its object onto another person, it becomes one more reinforcement of aggression. But properly canalized, it provides the biological root for the most human of actions, self-sacrifice.

The Breaking of Natural Patterns in Us

Biologically, assimilation and reproduction represent the conquest of space by protoplasm. When life rises to the level of tool-using consciousness, space is also conquered by the products of life—technology. When consciousness rises to the level of history, the spread of our species also conquers time; the awareness of this fact is the birth of language. The ultimate form of language is to define in poetry or legend the meaning of community as shown by "intercourse," social or sexual.

In the takeup of nature into history, as biological necessities are derailed into inappropriate functions, aggression (natural when directed at the bully) is institutionalized into subjecting the weaker. We reverse Vergil's imperial maxim to read, "To spare the *proud* and put down the *conquered*." The crown of our self-understanding, language, is perverted into pretending that the weaker is a threat, or that our aggression is to his interest. In the counter-functionality of the mass media, our ultimate function of understanding ourselves is corrupted into the ultimate perversion of deceiving ourselves.

Overpopulation with its attendant aggression overloads the very environment we were trying to secure; technology by its side compounds the damage. The beginning of a cure comes by our empathy with the childhood of the race in its instinctive revulsion at needlessly destroying a tree or an animal. We must then bring the needs of the environment into the turning-points of our life—precisely where the biological needs of the organism come to the fore, in actuality or symbolism.

The Restoration of Natural Order: A New Concern

A new concern is being built into our muscles and imaginations—the green revolution. If we're raising a family, own a woodlot, run a regulatory agency, we'll try to make it a model. But of course the real problems are on planetary scale: reversing pollution and exploitation, city and country planning, extending wilderness areas. International treaties with UN sanctions are needed. In the meantime a multiplication of voluntary groups like the Sierra Club is required—the more political the better, here is where politics can't go wrong. Right now we can start looking for men and money to restore the defoliated Vietnamese jungle.

Conservation in America, which had reached a liberal deadlock with the last national parks, in the last few years has cut deeper into our psyches. Rachel Carson made DDT a political issue, offshore drilling made oil a political issue, Ronald Reagan made trees a political issue. George Orwell saw that the sexual act would become a political act. Berkeley made nonviolence ecological; Frank Bardacke said, "Don't throw stones, they are parts of our mother." Nobody has the globe patented. The American Indian will have the last word, who shows up from time to time to remind us that even he is only the tenant of the land; the Great Spirit can bring himself to shake the ground and drop the fire because he knows that the Indian who upholds his peace will be able to survive.

Where suffragettes used to chain themselves to streetlights, it's more important for people to watch housewives chaining themselves to redwoods on TV. When the damage is done it's done; here massive civil disobedience most clearly has right on its side. Eventually the law must forget about ownership and come around to the principle that birds, mountains, waterways are nobody's private property but God's. *Earth and the Tree of Life rooted in her have a prescriptive right to existence.*

Nothing so brings us back to our childhood, to our real selves, as remembering what kind of rocks used to form the streambed, which flowers came up first in spring. Nothing so brings home to us the existence of different peoples as the apprehension of a different landscape in a Japanese print. For me the war really means a country stay at Nam Dinh, sitting outside a guest-house on the Red River (October 6, 1967), stranded by explosions at moderate distance and anti-aircraft fire. The noon air has the feel of a very hot season now mostly passed by. Earlier, children had been swimming the other side of the river, and bare-legged girls slogging through the paddy; now they are resting and listening to the radio. Two house-boats with floppy striped sails are moored upstream, bicyclists below are going across a bridge with bamboo handrail. A girl from the commune is going by me to wash the dishes in the river. (The guest-house is equipped with a new-style privy, and none of us Americans are getting dysentery.) Irrigation sloshes behind me in the banana grove where our camouflaged jeeps are parked, surrounded with big orange iris-like flowers in pots. Water lilies are floating at the river's edge. The Western eye must refocus to see that the thickets alternating with rice paddies are all bamboo, in dozens of species. Two dogs are playing beside me in the banana tree's shade, and golden sparrows hardly bigger than hummingbirds dart at the blossoms. Cooperation between nature and the works of man; a variation on the theme of a Vermont river-meadow, something quite different the planet had up its sleeve.

The power of the environment to resist our depredations is indirect and long-term: cutting off the supply of something we need to live. While the rivers still run clear, we must grit our teeth and go into the offices of men who think us fools, to make our plea for living things. The Greeks set temples where they were aware of gods already existing, as at Delphi. Benedictines picked abbeys with an eye to agriculture, sanitation, landscape. But Terra is our temple, our abbey. When the burning of fossil fuels or the tarring of the surface disrupt her breathing and heat-balance, we just have to start phasing out our cars and jets. The spiral of evolution points ahead to true fulfilment of the most archaic Stone Age spirituality, when civilization has melted invisible back under a restored forest.

chapter TWO

Peace Revolution: Renewal of Community

While physics and biology contain real knowledge constantly increasing, what are called psychology and sociology blur over old insights and don't replace them with a comparable body of knowledge. The understanding of human nature by any society is concentrated in the events where it first became aware of itself. Each generation is lucky if it reaches its parents' level of that understanding. As midwife of the future, it has also to affirm something radically new; but it affirms the new thing *about* the free humanity it first saw through old texts.

The Social Orders and Their Breaking

The biological needs taken up into our freedom are also spread out into social institutions. These are the necessary background of our self-understanding, but also the scene where the warping of natural orders goes furthest.

Within each social grouping there is created an oppressed class of victims—which by that fact is potentially the bearer of the future.

The family. Persons linked to us through begetting are our primary extensions into space and time, extra hands we can count on as our own. Through food-getting and reproduction we give birth to our own community, which holds more land than we could by ourselves. So also in time; my father is the living voice of the past, my son the hope of the future.

In the communication gap between parents who've accepted the challenge of affluence, and the young who reject the lavished gifts, the family generates two oppressed groups: the *retired* and the *young*. (It's not so clear to me as to some women that women are oppressed; but in following chapters I suggest some elements of their liberation.) Grandparents are baffled at the new generation conflict, and at their exclusion from it. There aren't any proper rooms for them in the new homes being built by a mobile class; they can't claim any longer to speak with inherited authority. The young have organized themselves; it would take a new Confucius to organize the old.

The working team. A father can hardly teach his son a job any more, cheated of a creative vocation himself and beginning to forget it. He simply identifies with current disorder; the young can see only hypocrisy and compromise. Paul Goodman, who found a big lack of manly jobs for the high-school graduate, chronicles the progressive disillusionment of the filling-station attendant.

The prostitution and powerlessness spread all up the

working scale; overpaid executives are equally unsure of their jobs and prisoners of the System. The System is prisoner of itself. Personal fulfilment exists only in rare pockets on any level. But there is a graduated injustice of reward, which Marxist analysis correctly sees as producing the victims of *workers and unemployed*. In America, where the grossly victimized are a minority, the viciousness of the System lies in its inability to resolve poverty and exclusion for that minority; in its massive projection of victimization overseas; in its dehumanizing effect on all levels at home.

The community of knowledge. The bond of consciousness between past and future is the University, the weakest link in the chain of oppression. It victimizes a class of *students*—the increasing percentage of our young people who go there, and find it unresponsive to their hopes of vocation, and collusive with the State.

Professors of language or biochemistry are distressed to see ill-informed students, Marxists or blacks, demanding seats on committees. They want no complicity in this overthrowing of the standards of competence and truth. But they hadn't previously confessed or noticed their complicity in an overthrowing of oppressed populations, their collaboration with agribusiness, slum landlords, mass media, makers of war. The University of California was the prime contractor for the hydrogen bomb. The students, groping for community, try to push back to medieval control by teachers and learners, before the faculty had gone into politics, and was replaced as owner of the University by politically appointed administrators.

But there's no way the University can wholly screen

out professional excellence in teachers and students. Competing schools of thought keep recognizable standards alive. The life of the sciences, arts, professions is objective enough so that from time to time actual competence breaks through. Thus Noam Chomsky, from his sanctuary at the Massachusetts Institute of Technology, has been the most responsible critic of professionals who abdicated responsibility.

Social classes. Groups of the same ethnic or cultural background should ideally be so bound up with a vocation or a vision of the future that they don't want to trade places with anybody. In Europe, most people wish to retain their own language, cuisine, and opera house; they're uninterested in emigrating. But there are only a few signs that every Akron is becoming a Vienna. Our immigrants sloughed off the best they brought, retaining vulgarized customs and churches less as a bulwark against assimilation than against black competition. Russia maintains varied peasant roots over against mass culture; we were uniquely unfortunate in the slave trade which built a *victim black class.*

Equality with functional differences between classes must grow organically. If it's organized from above, as often in Russia, the motive is manipulation. The translation of "separate and equal" is "separate and unequal." Autonomy of local groups sounds dandy until we translate it as "States' rights," the label for racist control of suppressed ethnic groups. Federal intervention in the South once appeared the helping hand of justice—until we saw that its purpose was building a united front at home to strengthen the hand of intervention overseas. Still, if

States' rights people should take their slogans seriously, they'd build blacks and whites into a real regional community, using Confederate buttons for draft-resistance. The Southern Conference Educational Fund (SCEF) calls its paper, the most effective voice for justice there, *The Southern Patriot.*

The State and its usurpations. From the city-state to now, political government has more and more englobed other forms of power—economic, military, police, communications, knowledge, medical, service. The State that sums them up plays a double role. So far as men are exercising genuine professions, the State harmonizes them. But so far as profession and natural orders have been broken by pollution, war, and alienation, the damage is done through the impersonal institutions which make up the State. A social institution, without the individual's conscience, forgets its original purpose. Individuals at fault begin its corruption and assent to it; but the corrupted institution has an inner demonic life of its own.

Political groupings are the organization of people on the basis of power. As long as institutions are defined by self-interest, they will conflict. A just distribution of power seems on the level of power unrealizable. Centralized power converts autonomy into satellites. The British Empire looked like a self-liquidating imperialism—until we saw that its former control, like that of the French, was mostly taken over by the economic control of its daughter, the American Empire. Western imperialism has created around the world a bloc of *oppressed nations.*

The best hope would seem to lie in a system of stable self-respecting states both protected and restrained by law.

But success on one level precludes success on a more important level. Our assimilation of white immigrants raised insurmountable barriers against the black. Our success in creating a zone of affluence here walls us off from the Third World—and our own dropout kids. Anything goes to defend that wall.

The State is indispensable in maintaining certain kinds of organization, and any substitute will turn out to be the State again in a different form. But the disorder centered in its activities is so high today that it threatens to tear down the whole fabric of institutions built into it, through environmental decay, class or international warfare, psychological collapse. And there isn't any merely political organ inside the framework of the State which can effectively criticize or redirect its course. The dilemma of the State as a self-destructing artifact can only be solved by changing the terms of the problem. The escalation of technology has made critical a need which always existed: an institution where people are organized on some basis other than power. A community.

The Cry for Community

As the State came into being regardless of the approval or disapproval of individuals, it will also so continue. Since it's the scene of the broad trend to violence, the form of authentic effort is searching for a place where that trend is reversed. This conclusion has either an anarchist or a religious tonality; for it means that a fully committed and realistic person can't make politics the heart of his struggle for justice. The center must be somewhere

else. Since the State has a big power of persuasion to re-
cruit well-meaning persons into its purposes, new community is always built through a minority. When the majority come in, the community is already far on the way to
fossilization; we just hope that the seed of creative dissent
is growing in it.

The institutions which make up the State, even when
functioning at their best, rest on coercion. The only
grounds of unity remaining is voluntary membership. The
State can claim our loyalty when on balance it's beneficent
or neutral. When it threatens basic orders, in everybody's
interest it must be resisted—in such a way that new breakage doesn't occur. The strength and balance to do this
can't come from an individual, much less from the State,
but only from a voluntary community with roots in the
past, reversing violence by reconciliation.

Each profession and art—much more the State—has a
built-in bias for itself. Beyond them all there is needed an
institution whose only bias is humanity, organizing a
broader base of people on a higher level—a tradition of
community. Its history is a fourth level of order above biological, social, and personal.

The only person we can trust is one who's reliably
undertaken to make our interests his own, or to discuss
conflict of interests before he acts. We can hire an em-
ployee to do this only in certain areas. But a man knows
when he comes home from work that the house will have
been cleaned, the children's quarrels settled, dinner
begun; a woman knows her husband will come home from
work. So the only institution we can commit ourselves to
without holding back is one which asks us to subordinate
our interests to other people—because we know it's mak-

ing the same request of them. Only it can claim trust from outsiders or count on indefinite growth. Because it considers its self-preservation secondary to the interests of outsiders; that is, it doesn't recognize the status of being outside. Only by pushing this single principle through to the end can it break out of the trap of becoming an immortal artificial person without conscience.

The Church as Inheritor of Community

On the wrong side of the fabric of history, dark brutality is the solid weave, and the gold is meaningless loose ends. Mostly like any seamstress we've got to do grubby painstaking work on the back side of the goods. But every once in a while we must turn the cloth over to see where we're going. Then the intended pattern emerges, a purposiveness bigger than individuals.

Like other natural growths, history on the planet has structure, grain. The growing edge of its development passed from the eastern Mediterranean through the Roman Empire to Europe. Along this axis, man's potentialities have been magnified both for good and for evil; the State, and the culture set inside it and against it, have achieved maximum development. Thus it was Europe (in part through her daughters, America and Russia) which introduced the rest of the world to the scientific method of achieving truth; but which also imposed its own culture and control on the other continents through political, religious, economic imperialism.

Being a free person in a free society means being a maker of images across time—symbolic forms defining our self-understanding and handed down through generations. In the Western tradition, free persons first appeared in the relatively democratic city-states of Greece and Israel, behind which no historic records were continuously preserved. Both saw dimly, in prophecy and myth, that man was slated to pass beyond freedom to love. The New Testament, drawing from both under the totalitarian Roman Empire, records the full realization of that possibility.

Beside Oriental teachers of wisdom, the Hebrew prophets and Jesus are both more realistic about the world's injustice, and more concerned to reduce it through genuine community. But if they set the standard for a coherent evolution, every society (like every individual) must have some intuitions of the same excellence. Even through the haze of Buddhist legend and our ignorance, we feel that Gautama illustrated in his society the same concern for individual integrity as Jesus in ours.

The meeting of Western and Eastern spirituality is an easy hope; but such things don't happen without conflict and suffering. The place where Christianity and Buddhism are coming into actual contact is Viet Nam. Far beneath the war, two courtesies are meeting under secular disguise. The reality of their rapprochement is measured by the fidelity with which the best people of both sides hold to their commitments in the face of murder and betrayal.

The paradoxical institution, which grows by not having a self-interest, must in the end be called the Church, collecting the threads of the ancient world for us. Each of our life-stages gets its real meaning only through solidarity with the historical Jesus—now in the crisis of our revolutions more than ever before. The element of "apology" in this book, justification for fidelity to our tradition, is spread out through the chapters which follow.

The Church's Case of Amnesia

It was possible, and foreseen, that the Church would forget its purpose as universal institution. Like everything possible, it happened. In every other institution, power and self-interest are built in by definition. Therefore the Church, whose definition is to reject power and self-interest, is open to more complete exploitation than any other. Whenever it loses its character as community by becoming coercive or violent, it takes on the same ambiguity as the State—that is, it becomes part of the State. The most obvious corruption is the take-over of the Church by segments of the State, which use its moral authority over individuals to further their purposes.

The Established Church in America is uniquely vulnerable to the application of its own principles; for through immigration it's become a mirror of the world scene. The perennial corruption of the Church has assumed definitive forms in America today: the *heresy of idolatry,* pinning our hope to an exploitative State; the *schism of denominationalism* which no longer believes even in its own alleged principles. So the conditions under which alone its message can actually be spoken or heard are renewal and reunion: *radical nonviolence* and *radical ecumenism.* The Reformation standard of a "standing or falling Church"—namely, the preaching of justification by faith alone—went back to Paul; nonviolence and unity would mean a penetration back to Jesus.

The silence of the American Church in face of violence is the other side of the Voice of America. What keeps the denominations separated and silent is the identical moral rift which has opened up in each; are people willing to make excuses for murder or not? The theoretical top-level ecumenism of the Consultation on Church Union (COCU) is seen to be irrelevant even by the gradualist liberals; and so they've directed their remaining moral concern into tentative urban reform—all that their constituencies will swallow.

Each denomination played its role in creating the America we know—Massachusetts Congregationalism, the Established Church of the central states, Methodism and the sects of the frontier, the Catholicism of the immigrants. As violence is destroying the American synthesis, the denominations, having served their function, are being melted down into something new. Our best model is still the new Church of South India, whose radical reunion sprang from the most deeply oppressed sector of the nation of nonviolence.

At the base of the dying trunks of Church and State, beside the deadwood are springing the vigorous root-suckers of liberation and renewal. Nobody knows how long they'll be able to grow and organize, flowering from the perennial root, before the burden of power is laid on them. *Now,* while the world can't recognize them, are being deposited the first woody layers which will let them bear weight—and also determine their future shape. Today is the only day we can count on to build better safeguards against injustice into new institutions. But if we have had to look for life elsewhere, so have millions of others. A generation of despair and hope must rewrite its constitution.

The Restoration of Community: A New Covenant

The Church would be useless to the State for take-over unless in some sense it *is* the Church, producing in each generation lives of saints. Mostly its actual work goes on outside the Church so labelled. It must recognize Marx as a prophet of justice, even though he failed to see the temptation of his socialism to fall into power-seeking. The apostles of nonviolence are precisely the Church of Jesus incognito. Whenever a person grasps the original principles of its founding, ripples spread out from him indefinitely far down to history afterwards.

In spite of genocide against the red man, the black man, and the yellow man, America has been the refuge of Protestantism and protest. The moving frontier spread across the continent seeds of a genuinely new way, even though now heaped over with rubbish. Along the arrow's flight marked out by the Mayflower Compact, there's laid on us the duty to form a *new covenant of humanity* here, suitable for export.

The cry for peace and liberation, even when self-centered, is the seed for renewal and reunion of the Church. The shoe is on the other foot; the existing denominations are to be seen as part of the Church of Jesus *to the extent* that they let the new wind blow through them. Pope John XXIII pointed to the unity of God's people; we can't see yet how far his church or others are willing to follow. The essential marks of the Church incognito are service to need, resistance to evil, openness to difference; in the end also it needs to take off its incognito and be seen for what it is.

Our inner freedom and our biological nature are partners, mutually raising each other up. Our first act of restoration for the planetary environment will remove inner psychological blockages, and help us work towards further restoration. The same mutuality exists between the individual and the community. Each person is conscious in his personal inadequacy, the weakness of his left hand, of needing to rely on the community which his right hand is planting and watering.

Church history thinks to set us the dilemma of choosing between the separated sect set over against the faults of society, and the universal Church identified with them. But what we see springing up in the actual present is a Church scattered through all countries; universal and radical; Catholic and *therefore* set over against each society it finds itself in. Our membership in that Church—our adherence to the revolution—revives the Stoic dream, first seen under Alexander's universal empire, of becoming citizens of the planet at large. By that membership, distrust is actually beginning to break down. Over against the manipulated United Nations Organization, there is growing up a counter-community, an United People's Organization.

We must insist on a community universal in space and time—a rising bread in all lands leading back to the past of each society's original self-awareness. And in fact the golden sunflower of our inner awareness begins to turn its face upwards. The great religions interlock. From Buddhist India came the nard with which the Messiah was anointed, the jewels in the better world of Isaiah and Plato and John. The cult of the hibernating and resurrected bear, our brother who tastes the honeycomb, was brought by the Pennsylvania Germans (and attached to the woodchuck) in an America where bear-totems had crossed the Bering Straits.

Somewhere within the movements of our time, reveille is being sounded for a new level of humanity—new, but also the realization on global scale of an old level. Over against the Communist Manifesto, which sets mankind at war with itself, another trumpet calls out that the enemy is within all and external to all: "Peoples of the world, unite." It can't be done in the framework of business as usual, golf as usual, church as usual, draft as usual, school as usual. Lifelong commitment, resistance, persecution, comradeship are in the cards—as we were told from the beginning.

chapter THREE

Inner Revolution: Renewal of Integrity

Even after we trace out each root of a man or woman in the soil of biology, each tendril in the woodland of society, we haven't touched the person's center. How shall we think about the power by which we become aware of our niche in space and time, and to that extent escape it; aware of our faults, and are so far liberated from them?

Our Freedom as Linkage Between Nature and History

Man perfects the tendency of the universe to turn things inside out. To grasp his inner space we must start from an overview of the outer space he organizes—for example, sitting here on the yellowing spring grass of the Berkeley hills on a windy afternoon, looking down over the University, and west across the Bay to the Golden Gate Bridge. Hidden behind Mount Tamalpais is the valley of fog that waters the Muir redwood forest. I could about sail a paper airplane onto the roof of Cal library, with its excellent classical and Semitic collections. Behind me, on the other side of a fence which forbids loitering in the name of the Regents, is the cyclotron; they are discovering things about the elementary particles we should be let in on. South across the Bay the smoky trail of a jet is taking off over the white buildings of the city to Hawaii, Tokyo, Bangkok.

Every square foot has human fingerprints on it—a double set. On one hand, adaptation of the environment for knowledge and use, as in the elegant catenary of the bridge, imposing significance on its cliffs like a Greek temple. On the other hand, deterioration. Old accounts describe a crown of redwoods around this bowl of earth and water, now replaced with weedy Australian eucalyptus. The garbage dump in the Bay has grown, balancing the unsightly rectangle of Treasure Island naval base. A big tin can sitting on the Richmond hills undoes the work of the bridge. Choking white feathers sprout from the factory chimneys of Oakland and West Berkeley; around them huddle the two-bedroom stucco manors of the ghetto, cramped in by the polluted bayshore and the elevated transit tracks. Smoke trails up from a thousand cookout campfires of the white occupying force in the hills. Two freighters are putting out to sea from Port Chicago and Alameda, I suppose carrying materiel to Cam Ranh Bay.

This network of information and control and destruction, the product of only a hundred years, is the outer shell of the elastic elusive thing we're trying to grasp—the collective and individual freedom at the nodes of the network, sprawling over space and time, turning inwards in knowledge and blindness. Just out of sight are Sproul Hall steps, where a revolutionary government one day may set a plaque marking Mario Savio's place in the Free Speech Movement of 1965. Somewhere in the preternatural smog overlaying Oakland, the all-American city, is the Induction Center where so many of my friends were busted in fall of 1967—to exchange Johnson for Nixon. It would seem as if the use and abuse of freedom were inseparable, two faces of Janus, two sides of a coin. But something in us cries out that the coin is only sandwich-silver, there must be a way to split its halves.

A week after I made those notes, Sheriff Frank Madigan's blue-coveralled deputies were running amok through the streets shooting hippies. Brigadier General Bernard Nurre called down a helicopter strike on students and bystanders with lingering CS—riot-control canisters diverted from Saigon. And in this early spring of 1970 *everything is closer together;* the cushions between motive and act, act and result have been taken away. We say to our brother "thou fool" and we become in fact his murderer. Technology instantly translates our disrespect for nature into wasteland. There aren't any wilderness areas or passive societies which can simply absorb our hatred. By the same token, a blow aimed at our brother strikes us. The mass media impartially record both the violence done to exploited populations, biological or social, and the excuses by which we explain it away.

We're faced with the primordial riddle that good and evil are brothers. A riddle is a description of something familiar, so accurate that it becomes strange again:

> As round as an apple
> As deep as a cup
> And all the king's horses
> Cannot pull it up.

But even when we realize the answer, it doesn't explain how a *well* gets water at the bottom. And what is the water at the bottom of ourselves? Man is a walking riddle, a flesh-and-blood contradiction. But we can only see this because we already had the idea of a radical consistency.

We didn't invent our standards of excellence, or the severity of the judgments that get passed; we inherited them from Greek tragedy, Hebrew prophecy. The Buddhist world will find them in its own past. Those first seers didn't invent them either; by fresh insight they saw historical laws operating, in their present or the future. Until recently, retribution was delayed long enough so that men could think of the standards as merely ideal, the judgments as only symbolic. Today both the visionary and everyman have adequate ground to fear the judgment of God as the billy clubs fall on the skulls, as the fish die in the polluted Bay. But if everything that can happen will happen, then we must also reckon on the sanctifying grace of God as a daily possibility. Of course, when we see the wagon-track dipping down into the flooded streambed, we look around for every other possible route first. Salvation is the last resort.

Of all the failures the University can be charged with, the chief is seldom made, especially by revolutionaries. It gives very few of its students a foothold in their own past —the classical and Hebrew world. Better translations from Greek are available than ever before, but students don't treat them as seriously as translations from Sanskrit or Chinese—languages we *know* we won't learn. Young people who do feel the unique value of these texts are shunted into minute pedantic studies. Where is the man to whom Achilles or Jeremiah is the model for his own excellence?

Our incautious extensions drag us down. The down-payment on a house, job-offers, the threat of conscription, the fear of failure, our first success, channel us in improper directions. Through passive assent to the management of society by the mass media, creativity withers. Homogenization denatures protest into stylish marketable consumer-products; hippy ateliers mass-produce peace symbols for New York tourists. "Revolutionary work" means running the mimeograph in a scrubby office—a faithful caricature of the business world. If idealism attracts us into the life of service, we see that the only slots available—as social workers, clergy, teachers—are constantly liable to takeover by malfunctioning institutions for their preservation.

The American businessman puts eighteen hours a day into making himself invulnerable: work and play, office and home, ruthlessness and charity, all fits together. On the other side we're reproached by the voluntary hardships of a Che Guevara to make himself a true revolutionary, "the highest type of human being." What can we put beside all this single-mindedness? We all know that each step in our past could have been firmer, without our typical inattention, conflict of motives, shortcuts, laziness, tendency to self-defeat. But how do we know this? Above all *from the examples of those who've done better:* saints.

The Restoration of Humanity: A New Commitment

It's hard to see how past excellences could be improved on—sculpture, architecture, painting, polyphonic music, tragedy. That is, they can't even be equalled, since doing the same thing over again is no equality. The radical potentiality of the future is *actual novelties of human character,* with growing real influence on the world. A manipulative society wants us to believe that any reputation for consistency must be the result of a public relations campaign. But the saint, even more than the philosopher or scientist, has a genealogy; he's reproducing, with appropriate variations, a type of character long ago invented. Some like Pope John have acquired wholeness by a childlike freedom from certain knowledge and doubts; others by feeding on them. The very existence of a post called Secretary General of the United Nations created a new character: judge among the Great Powers, servant of the human race. We come to see people as belonging to "our" society just so far as we actually stand beside them; the citizenship rolls of community cut across all boundaries, languages, centuries.

It would seem as if in so bureaucratic a society, where information is thought the uniquely scarce item, change must be a committee product. But a committee can't come up with the life-style, or the use of words, which move men to new action. What Herbert Marcuse calls the "repressive tolerance" of the system is a careful screening out of all the signals from the past, from nature, from overseas, from the inner world, which would question the glossy finish. The moon-landing and war-reportage were packaged for unreality, complete with ads, to resemble Saturday morning comics. But in unpredictable moments of sanity the truth breaks through. The isolated prophet, filtering out of the information-Niagara precisely the critical items, once again puts together the figure of an actual human being.

The message going out across the oceans is that the need for integrity has given birth to integrity. *A new sanctity has been born.* A center of consistency in the sloshing tides; actual working energies directed to the rebuilding of nature and community, starting with ourselves.

The dogma that character must always be ambiguous came from the effort to maintain a fictitious private morality inside a manipulative mass society. But when the easy career ladder has been cut off, not by our choice but society's, the traps are no longer hidden. We may still exploit the revolution as a field of academic study, or as an excuse to lapse into old violence for a new cause. We may get too far ahead, lose the way, and retreat into conformity or fall casualty. But there's a position of dynamic equilibrium where the pulls from all those directions cancel each other out. We'd always been told that sanctity was forced on us, not chosen. Now we see that the whole breaking wave of history demands that balance from us—and makes it possible.

Men assume that moral action involves a choice between existing alternatives—that is, between two evils. But each dilemma should bring out the courage and creativity to invent an original alternative, to put the discussion on a new plane. We can't look for this to functionaries who haven't yet seen the situation on this denuded, colonialized, disoriented planet—much less the possibility of making their own creative response, again and again. The field is wide open. Nobody has thought to train for the marathon, and we incompetents who happened by are told by the judge to put on track shoes and wait for the pistol.

If this book differs from manuals of ethics, it's because no provisions for a double standard are laid down. Actually "ethics" or its translation "morality" is the wrong thing to be talking about, because both mean "habit." And we must break through both old habits and the habit of habit, to look at things always freshly. The excellence of the saint looks like habit to the outsider; but as the man or woman sees it, every time you wake up the same struggle must be gone through.

Traditional ethics assumed we already had a frame of reference—a profession, a bank account, a social status—and asked us to balance threats to that status against the demands of morality. But this meant that, long before it caught its moral man, he'd already made his basic choice —perhaps not quite beyond reach of revision. We have to start farther back and take up the burden of choosing, not our actions, but ourselves. We're not to work by a set of rules, but by a vision of the character which is the true center of renewal. And we're not faced with a variety of situations which may, or may not, alter rules; the situation is a global fact. The correct thing doesn't run at right angles to our interests, so that compromise or renunciation is called for; we're asked to step through a false consciousness to recognition of our real long-term interests— and those of the planet, and of our great-grandchildren crying out to remember them. We're not up against a conflict of interests but a question of fact: which things build true order and which don't?

When one man blows the trumpet, that's ego-gratification; however ingenious his publicity, what he begins will eventually die. We recognize the right time to follow when the signal is given not by man but by God— that is, by a turn of events which no individual began. Our wounds are the clearest sign. We can be sure that others will have felt what has scarred us so deeply, our training and talents weren't all that special. Of course some of them are trying to choke down that awareness. Since we don't want to despair of them, we have to say that a demonic smog has distorted their vision; dispelling it is our job.

The cry to demythologize old symbolism was untimely. "Whenever," a theologian asked, "do we read in the daily papers that angels or demons are the immediate cause of historical events?" Daily. We can't simply condemn as unredeemable our brothers who've been recruited into violent institutions; nor give saints of our age the personal credit we know they'll refuse. To pass beyond condemnation and hero-worship is to see history as the battlefield of more-than-human insurgencies of good and evil.

Older classics of spirituality show a thoroughly individual trip into inner space: Pascal's *Pensées,* the *Imitation of Christ.* Inner life in our time is blossoming in the common tasks of world renewal, as with a Bonhoeffer, a Hammarskjöld. The earthscape against which our work must be done looms clearer—above all through the vision of the Jesuit Pierre Teilhard de Chardin. The most urgent call to our following is sent out by another student of Ignatius Loyola, my friend and brother Daniel Berrigan, designing a brand-new spirituality through his loving battle against his State and Order.

The years which turn institutions once fresh into brittle caricatures of themselves are also the golden bowl to be filled with the water of life. Ignoring the pseudo-events by which the media distract us from realities, we make current needs so vivid that even our sloth can't ignore them. Refusing all Novocaine to deaden the days of our felon's sentence, we methodically build time. Under the spring sunshine of our careful attention, dormant branches bear sap. As we become aware of our solidarity with men and women in other times and situations, we slough off crippling limits; the skeleton, musculature, nervous system of an eternal community of love take shape. It spontaneously moves over to make room for us; Homer is modified by Shakespeare, and our gentleness makes up (we're told) what was defective in the sufferings of the founder. In the dark valley of our conformism and folly, as our eyes get used to looking, on every slope we see the fireflies of original lives lighting up. The galaxies of a new universe are being born.

The Stages of Our Liberation

By reversing the corruption of the elements of our life we turn back the chain of radioactive decay, and transmute our lead into light-giving uranium again. As the place where nature and history intersect, we are not so much to begin as to *become* the reconstruction of biological and social order. In the first place this involves a reconstruction of the Church. In her unique sacramental relation to the biological order, she can initiate a global reversal of violence; also she is the most effective lever to budge the other institutions of our society.

Any scheme of parcelling out our life will do which lets us get quickly down to work on its actual texture—the cloth where actual reweaving is done. The planetary demand for life will analyze itself in accordance with whatever divisions we adopt. Here I modify the Catholic scheme of seven sacraments, which form the necessary link between nature (in their concrete biological symbolism) and society (in their liturgical format and historic origins). Shakespeare's seven ages include items that the Church misses—vocation and the realm of the State, the pot-bellied justice and bearded soldier. I'm also influenced by Erik Erikson's scheme of eight stages of development; if each faculty isn't developed at its own right time, the person is permanently stunted. But I begin where he starts to end—at late puberty, when the individual for better or worse makes his own decisions, on the basis of equipment built into him through the family.

On the fixed biological groundbass of birth, sexuality, and death, a force going beyond nature and history is building each turning-point of our lives into a revolutionary sanctity. Our beginning is to formulate clearly the demands made by each period of life in the permanent new situation.

The demand for fidelity: a fresh start. As each individual in his birth repeats the birth of the species, by a symbolic rebirth he must take on the fidelity called for by history—from now on, a commitment to nonviolence.

The demand for love: sexuality. As sexuality continues the species, each person, through marriage or otherwise, takes on the job of building a few others into the most permanent possible example of stable community.

The demand for usefulness: vocation. As each person channels sexuality into creativity, we must redesign old vocations and invent new ones to push through the necessary tasks of the revolution.

The demand for justice: the problem of power. Aggression organizes people in a society of coercion, the State. Over against that imperfect justice, the individual must give a higher commitment to the principle of community through voluntary assent.

The demand to help: service. The most expensive form of community is availability to the needs of others. This universal ordination to human service, a waiting on table, is the most basic novelty of the New Testament.

The demand for hope: falling casualty. At another stage the tables are turned, and the waiter must be waited on. Our conduct when in casualty status measures the genuineness of that community which we claim is constituted by failure.

The demand for joy: the feast. Both the individual body and the body of the community are maintained and built up by the act of assimilation. In the context of the festival, all our phases and roles are celebrated in their final definition.

The Source of Renewal

Our individuality is marked off by our intersection with every other individual we've met or read about in books; we're a child of the actual community of the human race. So the renewal of the Church goes reciprocally with individual renewal; both the creativity and the flaw of man's freedom go deeper than any individual.

Where does the cry for justice come from, the scattered groping actions for new life? How can it be explained that where violence cut deepest, the indestructible urge to decency reappears? that the revolution breeds critics of revolutionary counter-violence? Somehow we must say that men are constantly touched, if they're willing, by a standard of truth which goes beyond both the exploitation they resist, and the failings of the resistance; it's not bound up with any one class, cause, society. Since time along with space is one of the things that emerged in cosmic evolution, the permanent possibility of new life is deeper rooted than the time and place where we first meet it. Our more than globular universe can only be moved by a lever resting on some pivot outside it. And we don't reach the bottom of any historical movement until we see it in cosmic terms. Myth-making man, not knowing so much of either history or science as we do, has the advantage that he can seize both together in one hand. Our liberal education consists in following the clue of his language to express that fact beyond facts. In the end, to label the revolutionary who again and again subverts history into love, we haven't got any choice but to apply the old names of God to that Archimedes, who, from his fulcrum underneath the cosmic manifold, with infinite gentleness guides it into new life.

Since most people at most times can't push analysis of history to the end, we must leave a lot of room for coalition with all those who, for excellent reasons, can't claim they're working in the name of God. But, although that claim is of course constantly being perverted, failure to make it in *some* language will in the long run lead people to find a different God. We have to agree that God is a jealous God, if you don't end up with him you end up somewhere else.

When a new idea has been thought of, it's repeated a hundred times over. One civil rights demonstration, one national liberation front, one peace march, one ghetto rebellion, one student take-over, one demand for reparations produces an indefinite number of others. All the more then we should be looking, both in the daily papers and in our hearts, to see where and how somebody first makes the decisive breakthrough out of the delusional systems which have imprisoned us for so long. A new infusion of life across continents was implicit in the moment in the chapel when John Wesley felt his heart strangely warmed.

It's easy to be diverted into doing something less than is indicated. The highest threshold to be gotten over lies in front of the door of life. It takes a man or woman of exceptional simplicity to go right up to it without being distracted. That consistency doesn't happen all of a sudden, it lies at the end of a long road of self-purification. And when we get there, we see that this end is only a beginning. The revolutionary fresh start required of us is the common sense to begin at the beginning.

part II: The Demands of
Our New Life

chapter FOUR

The Demand for Fidelity: Going Through the Waters

Most people never quite finish being born, we're tied by an umbilical cord to stepmotherly institutions. When this girl on our street first went off to school, she knew a string was tied between her and the back doorknob, which got looped around blocks if she didn't come back the way she went. We can all learn from the tadpole, who after the bother of learning to swim opts for a new environment.

The normal case of a fresh start is with the young person just waked up from the impression that the policeman and postman are towers of morality. During the sixties, in that overlap period when residual childhood freshness sensitizes the dawning moral judgment, the prevalence of poisoning, murder, and intimidation stamped itself forcibly on him. Late maturing is always possible. Still, if middle-aged people during the Johnson years could read the morning body-count and not get sick over their fried eggs, what will they gag on?

Diagnosis of Complicity by the Young

The young protest first what hits them directly, computerization: being put on a punch card, segregated into dorms, destined for social security, pre-enrolled for Freshman Comp, conscripted by aging realtors. Concerned parents ask: How do I get my child off drugs, off the street, into a proper marriage, into a real vocation? The preliminary answer is always: Stop the war and the draft. That would only be a first step: it's necessary also to change the habits and institutions which made the war and the draft. But for the kids, the draft is conclusive proof what old people are about. If they join the National Guard to avoid shooting local patriots overseas, they're dispatched to shoot high-school buddies or put a bayonet into the blouses of their old dates.

A parent who still sends out remittances won't believe that the young are an oppressed class. But they've burned their bridges, and the long hair unacceptable in Peoria or Houston is only a sign of that break. Frank Madigan, the sheriff of Alameda County, explained that many of his deputies were newly discharged veterans, and so of course treated demonstrators as Viet Cong. Integration has finally worked. Since the children of the ghetto couldn't be brought up to suburban level, the children of the suburb went spontaneously down to theirs—instant niggers.

A gypsy generation rediscovering play can't take on joyless adult make-believe. The substitute society they've patched up seems in its least common denominator impoverished enough: sleeping around, living off the street, smoking grass, wearing long hair and freaky clothes, improvising Oriental mysticism, listening to rock bands. If they still insist on preferring it, their judgment on grown-up culture is all the more persuasive.

The white dropout ghetto, though its criticisms are just, is no Messianic community; it's still a Coney Island mirror of middle-class society. It's moved beyond the mind-expanding drugs, which short-circuit the neural tracks (probably with premature aging) back to the old pills that Mom drops up in the tiled bathroom on Magnolia Drive: uppers (amphetamines) for acceleration to public speed, downers (barbiturates) for slowdown to private sleep. Its promiscuity reflects the serial polygamy back on the hill, which in turn is the other face of Puritanism. Its dirt on the outside of hopefully beautiful personalities is intended as a turning inside out of suburban hypocrisy. Its lack of planning reflects the improvisation of bourgeois culture, the pyramiding of credit. The suburb refuses to see future collapse. The dropout world refuses to see any future at all—it's reverted to the expectations of the world's end in primitive Christianity. "They were saying on the street in L.A. there's going to be this big earthquake when the pigs come on heavy next month, and my mind was blown because I'm Aquarian, so man I split."

While little kids are being given Social Security numbers, and pedestrians licensed by the Motor Vehicle Bureau, in reaction a *voluntary proletariat* is being born. All ragamuffin seventh graders look like hippies; but when we see their folks driving an old Ford truck to the PTA from an out-of-town commune in their beads and bare feet —or delivering our mail—we realize the computer may not win after all. The other day this dropout I know delivered his girl friend's little boy baby (uncertain whether it was his own) and cut the cord; no father, no birth certificate, no census report, no draft card; just a baby.

Washing Off Our Brother's Blood

If in our own way we try to grasp the interior of complicity, we move back through our nerves into our spinal cord, out into tendons, muscles, bones. The circuitry of our brain is jammed on Nixon's the one and rather fighting than switching. The base of our spine aches from the waiting benches at Welfare. We feel the itch of a fungus infection in our crotch from the garbage-teeming shores; leukemia spreads in our radioactive marrow; our toes tread the pools of resin from the felled redwood. In our nostrils is the smell of burned flesh. Our lack of pigmentation shrinks us back into the shade like a pulled onion.

And there is dirt on our hands, I look at my own alleged priest's hands: the feel under our fingers of the napalm burns, scars from fragmentation pellets and buckshot, Che's blood in Bolivia, blood from the streets of Selma and Newark and Chicago and Berkeley. The word we ask to be told is, Wash off your brother's blood. We keep bugging our kids to wash their little hands. We dream of the tsunami wave sweeping away the mess we've made of our families and jobs. We take long showers. In the interior seascape of our guilty heart, the beach girl in her scraps of cloth slouches beside the prophet in his camel's-hair, both pointing back to childhood waters.

In our lack of a collective myth, we Americans can only turn back to the private myth of our childhood. Nothing since then has gone so well as the summer vacations in the cottage with faded shingles by the shore. Going off to college, getting married, changing jobs, sending kids to high school all seem temporary detours, after which we'll go back to the beach and everything will be as it was. Each of us is Huck Finn, sneaking out in the twilight to a rowboat tied up under giant willows. Our childhood memory-bank is all plugged in to our appropriation, or rape, of the virgin country.

We must find a way to cut moral losses, not throw good time after bad. A fresh start would not only renew the soil that the blossom of the future grows from; it alters the judgments we apply to the past. Every action carries two possibilities: being whittled away to nothing, and being built on. In prophetic justice we look to our children for wisdom; the times they are rapidly changing. The stable end-product of nostalgia can be repentance.

Our century, which has gone right and wrong in so many new ways, has made a great thing of fooling around on beaches. Before us I can only think of Xenophon's marines swimming bare-ass off their sea bivouac. The knotted bikini, named fantastically after our greatest guilt, is fetish for our compulsion to go back to the fig leaves of Eden and the great waters. Our associations with water are a primordial complex: return to play, return to the womb, evolution, getting clean, nakedness and procreation, submission to death, washing off the death of guilt, drowning, return to the surface in the seafoam of resurrection. John Wheelwright summarizes in his elegy ("Fish Food") for Hart Crane, suicide by drowning:

The sea's teats have suckled you, and you are sunk far
in bubble-dreams, under swaying translucent vines
of thundering interior wonder . . .

No images will undercut these. We can only go back behind Cain and Abel by washing off our brother's blood.

Making a fresh start isn't rejecting sin and guilt (not
in our power) but accepting the burden of guilt. When
faced by the United Fruit Company, Dow Chemical, the
chainsaw in the redwood forest, Forest Lawn, the Central
Intelligence Agency, the RAND Corporation, the Oakland Housing Authority, Richard Daley's bullies, the
John Birch Society, our cue is to say, "There *by* the grace
of God go I." Our only strength is the forgiveness in
which we embrace a President or Presidium as brothers,
recognizing no hatred or violence of theirs as alien to us—
and at the same time resisting to the death the dark powers which have colonized them.

The Condition of Our Fresh Start:
Refusal of Conscription

The planetary strike invades our split-level bedrooms
in the dropping out of their children, which, even at its
least responsible, reflects a *non-negotiable demand for
fidelity*. Since fidelity only settles into a consistent state
over years, our beginning is just the initial condition of
new life. Even though children of Quaker or revolutionary families may never undergo a crisis of redirection, and
even though older people may also take the new route, *the
situation of the young determines the moral condition of
our fresh start*. Young men from eighteen to twenty-six,

the type of heroic humanity in Greek art, have become once again our moral leaders.

The modern State can't allow the precedent of letting citizens drop out unpunished; it has to keep up pressure for conformity in *some* area. Precisely that area must be the scene of our fresh start. A modern reader of George Fox's *Journals* is puzzled that his confrontation with Establishment came on the issues of wearing his hat in court and not taking an oath. But Caesar's illegitimate claims were only symbolic in those simple days. The pressure for religious conformity wasn't burdensome; even Fox couldn't perceive the error of slavery; he needed to offer his cheeks and back only to the violence of individuals. The American State applies greatest pressure, by prison and loss of civil rights, in the area of conscription, forced by its own imperial logic to provide the peace movement with a permanent organizing issue. Repeal would destroy U.S. foreign policy by opening the door to a massive anti-recruitment campaign. Nixon's campaign promise to end the draft will turn out to be a façade for continuing it— perhaps within a more widespread regimentation into Youth Service. Here young men, led by Fox's Friends, inevitably made their stand. In any foreseeable future here, *the regular moral demand of a fresh start is refusal of conscription.*

It might seem as if nonviolence were a functional specialization; we need some people to fight wars, others to protest them. It's true that a society needs garbage-collectors—but only a certain number. But there's no rational way of determining how many soldiers we need; the threat felt from a foreign power varies in proportion to the effort deployed to meet it. The maintenance of armies by males presumes women and old people incapable of forming rational judgments about their own interests.

In a society where not all are fearful and not all courageous, the initial task is not to abolish the military, but to reduce its level by subtracting oneself and others from it. If nobody volunteered, the country already would be invulnerable. And the refuser committed to the lifetime risk of peace-making isn't taking any easy way out. All countries are now so interlocking, that a general fear-level exists; my decision to spend time reconciling rather than fighting reduces it, so that afterwards *all* parties are more secure than before. The strength of our pullout lies in the Establishment's guilty awareness of its own contradictions; it hires moralists to reduce the violence-level at home, and imprisons them for reducing it abroad. The young men's unanswerable ultimatum is: we resist the draft in the name of nonviolence, or in the name of violence we join the revolution.

Does this necessary form of *our* fresh start have any relevance for oppressed communities—Latin Americans, blacks, Asians? Their obvious loyalty is identification with their own revolution; how could they go beyond it? After the death of King, the black nonviolent movement here is in full disarray. The best Latin Americans seem united behind revolution, as violent as needs be. Nonviolent resistance is having its biggest success in Czechoslovakia; but their special situation and national character seem irrelevant elsewhere.

This analysis, apparently discouraging, can be put in a sensational way: *America is the vanguard.* Just as our leaders claim, but in a slightly different way, our combination of residual freedoms with global power opens the chance for us to become leaders of humanity. Our young people have a unique universal vocation: separating themselves so clearly from exploitation that other youth around the world will have to follow their lead. They're a potential elite. It needs a crystal-clear ideology, a flexible but reliable organization, and an absolute commitment to the inner revolution of integrity.

As isolated examples of what could be done by millions, I think of Maximilianus, the African resister of A.D. 295, "I am not permitted to fight"; of Franz Jägerstätter, the Austrian Catholic peasant, lacking a single sympathetic soul beside him, who refused induction into Hitler's armies. I see a boy with long hair as one who won't have a regimented haircut. With gratitude I think of those now in prison whom I can't judge by any standard of morality, because in their quiet constancy they've become the standard I judge myself by.

The Resistance program succeeded beyond its dreams. As the actual organization melted into the landscape, largely through jail, thousands of young men (no doubt many with mixed motives) are simply not showing for induction or are refusing. The courts only prosecute a small percentage of cases at random, and even so are hopelessly behind. It's scary to see a breakdown of authority, because you don't know where it will end. Authority with all its task forces should have thought of that first. For all parties, amnesty alone—which we may well not get—could patch things up even for the time being.

Since our nation was populated in part by refugees from European conscription, we can hardly criticize men who take refuge in Canada or Sweden, or parents with young children who emigrate—even though we may regret their abandoning the most effective scene of action. Much less could any white man ask black youth to risk a Federal jail, lacking the verbal skills and social influence to have any hope of conscientious-objector status. As they melt back into the ghetto they join the global strike.

From one point of view, the authenticity of any act is only decided at the end of our life: how effectively did it move us towards a new way? From another point of view, the critical duty in the present has been to arrest our State in its criminally insane course of murdering a lovely people dedicated to its own culture. But—as that people also understands in its objectivity—compromise or untruthfulness *now* in the anti-war movement means a succession of new victims in the decades ahead.

The Original Discovery of the Fresh Start

Since we're faced with a planetary destruction of order, our individual fresh start is only made fully effective when built into a renewed planetary community. A community withers without roots in the past. To find common ground with our cultural cousins around the globe, we must dig back to the point where our roots interlace with theirs. You'd think Buddhists might look to the illumination of Gautama under the bo-tree; actually the Buddhists I know who take justice and ecology most seriously have moved three-quarters of the way over, they've gone Marxist. The Western book which underlies Marxism and all other social change presupposes a fresh start: *metanoia*, "conversion," a complete turnabout of our will and emotions which focusses them onto the single right object.

Shovelling off the alluvial deposits of magic, misunderstanding, compromise in century after century of ecclesiastical history, we dig underneath the dried riverbed to the perpetual undergound stream of mountain water. The original living cell of community, the little group of Jesus and his associates, crystallized around the fanatic preacher standing beside the waters. Jesus alone saw the meaning of what the baptizer was doing, and "was made sin for us," declaring his solidarity with Herod and Hitler. The records normally see the action as a mode of dying: "I have a baptism to be baptized with"; "as we are buried with him by baptism into death."

The Hebrews, like Thales the pre-Socratic, started from the swamp-cosmology of Sumeria. They saw it as re-enacted at every crisis, mythical or historical: creation, flood, crossing the Red Sea, crossing Jordan, return from exile. Each time there rises up wet and sleek from those waters a living community. Jesus' words and life define that emergence as a naturalization into the one fully legitimate commonwealth, a new community where the only sanction is love. His nonviolence in our world of technology run wild has become both necessary and possible for survival. As criticism discovers the uncertain areas of his biography, we move into the area where the documents allow no room for doubt—a new level of truth which their novel technique was specifically designed to record.

Jesus is unmarried; and dissociates himself from the self-punishment of John. He is a man of learning; and refuses the teacher's privileges. He is a popular leader; and rejects the compromises of realistic politics. He has deep psychological powers; and puts away from himself the role of wonderworker. He has unmeasured influence over his friends; and weans them away from him, refusing the labels by which they try to fix him. He believes in a power for which all things are possible; and regrets the sparrow's fall. He foretells war in which society and nature will perish; and rejects participation in the most just self-defense. He will not exploit the animal or vegetable realm; or do stones the violence of making them bread against their nature. He sets himself against imperial oppression of the poor; and also against counter-violence in their just struggle. By his example he puts maximum pressure on the others to follow; and refrains from all other pressure.

Every wave of exploitation beats against him and is dissipated into foam, because there's no part of him it can claim. He has passed through to the other side of death. Our only possible fresh start is identification with the principle he represents. That means entering the stream of history which flows from him. *Baptism is the permanently valid symbolic act by which we receive solidarity with Jesus' way of nonviolence.* Its intrinsic meaning, his well-attested character, ensure that always in the end it will lose any corrupt associations. It doesn't mark an exclusion but an inclusion; for it defines the only way the human race can live together.

Anointing with the Spirit

That immersion is obviously also a washing; when we understand the ancient bath, we see the connection with new life. There was hardly any water for bathing in ancient cities until the aqueducts of imperial Rome. After daily nude exercises, the Greek or Roman man smeared on low-grade olive oil, then clean sand, and scraped off the mass. A painted vase of olive oil was the prize for victors in the games. In the sun-baked Mediterranean this oiling, still followed by local athletes, is preferable to our constant baths; it keeps the skin supple, protects against burning and skin-cancer. In the ancient world, deficiencies in cleaning (and in extraction of the oil) were made up for by blending in scents—distillation of alcohol to carry perfumes was unknown.

At the rare ceremony of an actual bath in water, all the more important to restore skin-oils. Lower-class Arab girls in Beirut today, though very neat, seldom bathe from week to week; but on their wedding day undergo an elaborate bath with perfuming. Whenever Homeric heroes arrive at somebody's palace, they're bathed by the maids— perhaps country boys wouldn't know how to go about it. Then they're anointed with olive oil and dressed in a clean linen tunic.

The processions of the Parthenon frieze and Augustus' Altar of Peace show a free citizenry wearing their dress of office—white tunics or togas. Ideally they took a bath beforehand. (At the date of the reliefs, both Athens and Rome had become imperialist states, making propaganda out of democratic symbols; but the symbols are authentic.) The Greek names of the tunic (*chiton*) and of the best linen (*byssos*) are the Sumerian and Egyptian words for flax, brought in by Phoenician trade. Along with the fabric, the classical world also inherited from the Near East the civic context it was worn in.

Hebrew priests and kings (unlike earlier Near Eastern ones) held delegated authority, for they were answerable to the prophet, who enjoyed an inviolable status like the Roman tribune of the people. When they were consecrated for office, they probably took a bath, and were anointed (as still in Britain) and clothed in vestments which defined their office. Prophets shared the anointing.

When Jesus was seen as summing up the roles of king, priest, and prophet in an unexpected way, he was given all three offices under the title of "Anointed," Aramaic *Messiah*, Greek *Christ*. (He is also seen in Greek manner as a victorious athlete.) The elements of consecration are spread out through his life: the ritual bath, an anointing, investiture in the murex-purple cloak of royalty. All point to that death which confirms his Messianic status: "This Jesus whom you crucified, God has made both Lord and Christ."

The acts of passage through the waters and anointing are seen together as conveying the "gifts of the Spirit." There is a uniform Mediterranean physiology in which the word for "wind" (Hebrew *ruah*, Greek *pneuma*, Latin *spiritus*) also means "breath" and "principle of life." The *ruah* of God which moves on the face of the water is a pre-cosmic wind, thought of as his breath, which impregnates the deep into life. Later he breathes it onto the clay which he has shaped. So the ritual bath, which marks our birth into a new state of life, is taken as the point where we start breathing its atmosphere.

A community is seen as a bigger man animated by its proper breath or "spirit." Its "members" are limbs of his body, and are ascribed common descent, real or adoptive. Hellenes are descendants of Hellen son of Deucalion, survivor of the Flood; Israelites of Israel-Joseph. We're all sons of Adam. One trouble in America is that we can't revive the myth of Noah to give white and black a common ancestor.

Jesus' original ideological program, the Sermon on the Mount, represents his understanding of the fresh start which both he and his hearers have just made. Their baptism by John generated a new community inside Israel, where Jesus through his gifts emerged as leader. In its *esprit de corps* we come to live "in Christ" the principle of reconciliation, as previously we had died in Adam the principle of estrangement.

Murder is committed by the first sons of Adam; its result is Babel, many peoples with mutually incomprehensible languages. The community of Jesus is held together by a common spirit which puts the mutually understood tongues of brotherhood in every mouth. Communication through the shared language of dialogue is also the form of the new community invented by Plato.

Baptism and Confirmation in the Church

When under Constantine the Church was taken up into the power-structure, the phases of the ritual bath were separated. Baptism became a token of membership in the only society anybody could see, of which Church and State were two elements. Hence it was put as early in life as possible. (Constantine himself, the link between two ages, postponed baptism until he'd finished his necessary crimes.) The gift of the spirit became optional and was put around puberty.

The Reformation State Churches were in a dilemma; they were the religious phase of a total society, but they wanted to return to the principle that a person chose the new way of Jesus freely. But then there had to be a possi-

bility of his rejecting it—or choosing it in a way unacceptable to the established Church. They patched up the
dilemma by continuing infant baptism, and making
confirmation theoretically an acceptance in one's own person of what had been promised before by others. Soon that
reaffirmation became mostly formal. The total society was
broken instead by the appearance of dissenting churches
and then of skepticism, always against opposition. In the
end it was secular law, not canon law, that evolved the notion of tolerance—which for the first time since Constantine restored to the Church in principle its autonomy over
against the State.

But within any of the existing denominations today, as
in America, baptism is an infancy rite, introducing the
baby to the community. Confirmation or confession of
faith is a puberty rite of graduation from church school—
really of graduation from church. For we've evolved a children's religion, suitable also for those in second childhood,
patronized by adults principally to ensure attendance of
their kids in church school. Entrance into that religion is
no longer an act of separation from the world, but of identification with it.

The radical Reformation sects restored adult decision
to split from the world, preserved in theory by Baptists.
Their liberal clergy, hampered by tradition from making
immersion less than total, can dispense with it today altogether. But we face evils for which immersion is not too
great, but too little, symbolic expression. In their guerrilla
attacks on draft boards, the Baltimore and Milwaukee
Catholics used real self-drawn blood, real homemade napalm. If ever somebody in the Peace Movement is baptized, he'll actually get wet in some body of water—maybe

a Baptist tank. The bellbottomed trousers and army jack-
ets of our dropouts, with their cry for authentic drama,
point back to the old symbols—the white garment, can-
dles, procession. No need to refute their mythology that
the myrrh of Moses' anointing oil was psychedelic.

The early Church communicated a secret summary of
ideology to the candidates, and we should be working on
such a chain of slogans. The imposition of hands, begun
by the minister (a link with the global community in
space and time), should spread to the whole group with
the kiss of peace—what all humanity except Anglo-Saxons
do when they meet. Mutual acceptance, reciprocal subordination. We verbal types needn't be surprised if action
people, normally tongue-tied, respond in the languages of
play.

Adult Baptism as Normative

So far as the Church claims to be the nucleus of the renewed community, it must make commitment to itself an
adult affair. In the rapid social change we'll be seeing to
the end of time, each generation must decide for itself to
take on integrity. That was also how the Church began.
Of course people are growing up younger than they used
to, in the accelerated political consciousness of our high
schools.

In a stable society before scientific medicine, being
born was the biggest trauma when acceptance was most
needed. The later crises of puberty, marriage, vocation
were slid over or prearranged. Today with medicine and
natural childbirth, coming into the world isn't necessarily

to be propitiated by parents or child. But the infant baptism fastened onto us by medieval fear of death has robbed the Church of the proper way to manifest its own beginning.

The American Resistance has developed a symbolism of original power for young men to take the right road: the turn-in of draft cards. But it's an action vulnerable to the whim of the State to modify or repeal, like the incense on Caesar's altar. Then and now, resistance to Leviathan is the natural moral condition of baptism—but not a substitute. It's not available in the same way to women or older men, and doesn't operate on the same psychological level.

In our transitional period, most converts to a renewed Way have been baptized as babies by conformist parents in a conformist Church. Of course the new church is the daughter of the old; when it goes back to mother saying "War is murder" it doesn't want to shock, but to show how well it's learned its catechism. Still, as the Roman church suspects the form or intent of Protestant baptism, much more may we suspect the form or intent by which babies without conscience are accepted into racist exploitative societies. Out of the peace revolution is born an evangelism of actual sin and actual redemption—awareness of complicity and of liberation. Persons aware of coming into the community of new life for the first time should have the privilege of entering it—and by the means indicated in old books, in their subconscious desires. Instead of asking theoretical questions about validity, why not rather ask the person what (if anything) has happened? *For persons baptized as infants in established churches, the normal mode of taking on renewal will be conditional rebaptism.* Its vows should clearly define the meaning of recruitment into the nonviolent revolution of Jesus—what the Book of Common Prayer should intend by "Christ's faithful soldier and servant."

If America moves towards stable revolutionary Quaker-style families, the cry for "birthright" infant baptism would return soon enough. The danger will be that once again a way of life (however objectively correct) will be imposed on children without their wishes having been consulted. Of course people hope their kids will follow them in the peace revolution; but it can't be done in Maoist style by youth battalions, but only by availability of the option and persuasion.

Getting the Message Through Obstacles

How can the unionized blue-collar workers, ill-educated and TV-watching, be brought to see the unsatisfactory substitute for living that's been fobbed off on them? As the Resistance has struggled to push its convictions over apathy and bureaucracy, it's been driven out of Puritan shyness into ritual drama—the stylized vulgarity in the morality-plays of the San Francisco Mime Troupe, the Bread and Puppet Theatre. Few have bugged the churches so successfully as the guerrilla street liturgies of our own Dick York, of Viv Broughton's radical CHURCH in London. The Cranmers of our new age shall be Jerry Rubin and Abbie Hoffman, burning five-dollar bills at the Stock Exchange, milling in for peace, wearing revolutionary costumes to un-American committees, inaugurating pigs.

The Fresh Start as Rebuilding Community

As we dissociate ourselves from exploitation in the world, much more so in the Church, which we claim as seed of a new world. Since denominationalism marks the Church's powerlessness to throw off complicity, our baptism is a rejection of denominations. The precondition of reunion is our personal fresh start. As obedience to God implies disobedience to the State, so far as it's trespassing on his property, it also implies an act of *ecclesiastical disobedience,* so far as the Church has gone along with the State. The membership rolls of sixteenth-century Christianity don't make sense any longer. The only Church we can be baptized into is underground or underwater—the yellow submarine we all live in.

Nascent congregations are springing up from the community already there in the peace movement. History is gathering together children of the denominations who heard the message their clergy transmitted and rejected. The liberated Church will become visible when seminarians ask to be ordained in it, when people come to be baptized into the thing which is blossoming—precisely as a result of their adherence.

To swing the compass-needle of our psyche into line with the electromagnetic field of the cosmos may begin as an act of deprivation: the schizoid withdrawal which points to a new center outside claiming us; the auto accident which snaps old threads and makes us put the new together. But when we emerge finally from the waters and a dove brings the olive to our brow, if ever in our lives we should know what it means to be a man or woman. The first test of our fresh start is our freedom simultaneously to concentrate psychic energy into sexuality and to sublimate it into creativity. The next crisis is our non-negotiable demand for love.

chapter FIVE

The Demand for Love:
The Source
of Creativity

The chemist sees water as the fundamental liquid, and normal saline or wine as complex and derivative. So the Department of Philosophy line is that clear colorless consciousness is the normal state of ourselves. But the actual condition of our psyche is a spectrum of colored emotional states, where sexuality issuing into creation is predominate. In Hebrew the primary meaning of the verb "to know" is sexual, "And Abram *knew* Sarah his wife"; the intellectual meaning is gotten from this by abstraction.

Our relationship to other living creatures is floated on a sea of sexuality. We play a feminine-passive role over against the animals; like the female of their species, we admire the lion's mane, the peacock's tail, the stag's antlers, the cock's comb. Art today, as in early matrilineal societies, stresses female sexual characteristics; but our classic art is marked by statues of the naked standing male. We've derived from the animals the will to domination over fellow-males, which is extended to control over nature and magnified into mindless social institutions; but sexual domination needn't be so destructive.

The Derailment of Sexuality

The energy of sexuality tends to get invested in symbols, bank deposits of its gold. A handkerchief, a ring, a photo, places, odors. The nostalgia for childhood landscape or the reliable tune of the summer merry-go-round is projection of preadolescent sexuality. The psychic stirring which at a different place or time leads to overt sexuality can illuminate a scientific problem, push us into craftsmanship, remind us of a friend in trouble. The act of sex consummated is a psychic sanctuary to march out from and return to safely. Sublimation and fulfilment: poles of one magnet.

The interdependence of society reflects on the cultural level the biological necessity of intermarriage. The incest-taboo, the body's own awareness of harmful recessive mutations, spreads out positively into elaborate kinship systems. In early and primitive societies, the exchange of women, like commerce, is a bond tying neighboring communities together—the original civilizing influence.

The different wave-lengths of sexuality in men and women, which they can never tell each other about, are the psychic components of procreation. As the newly fertilized ovum imitates the first life in the primordial sea, our desire reflects a planetary tension in the eons of pre-life. The superabundance of our sexuality provides for the continuance of the species. And also the head of steam for all other creativity too; our best ideas come in the free play of dreaming. But if we let that engine run idle for too long it shakes itself to pieces.

When a society has become an end in itself and lost the assent of its supposed citizens, it begins advertising itself and manipulating them through technique grown autonomous. The Roman Empire advertised itself through its own power—coinage, inscriptions, the emperor, the army. The Middle Ages advertised themselves through their own civic and divine cult. Our society has to give people apparent freedom of choice; religious symbols have died, power must be pretended improper. So everything we want to sell has to be advertised through a woman's belly. It's remarkable that so many Americans can break through mystification and find the road to wealth and power.

A distorted culture cheats desire with unrewarding objects: a cat, a homosexual attachment, pornography, compulsivity. The derailment of sexuality, in its twisting of inner space, mirrors manipulation of the outer environment—and of the nature-peoples who inhabited it before we came along. Especially in America, destructive sexual tension is built up by the interracial affinities which are supposed not to exist. Eldridge Cleaver, during his years of celibacy on ice, analyzes the whole of our society as the forbidden liaison between the Supermasculine Menial and the Ultrafeminine, with the Omnipotent Administrator and the Amazon standing frustrated in the wings.

Marriage as Permanent Gene-Cell
of Revolution

The direct biological fruit of sexuality is childbirth, which tames it and transfers it to new objects. Its indirect cultural fruit has been called sublimation: a direct change from solid to gas without ever passing through the liquid state. Sublimation normally appears as the creativity of a profession, learned by apprenticeship, and continuing society by cultural rather than genetic inheritance. It's important to keep the two channels distinct: not to try and teach your wife everything you know, not to make love to your students.

Each phase of the revolution will only blossom out of a stable cadre, convinced about what must be done, and ready to wait five, ten, twenty years until the right moment for action. The family is the primary cadre. If we can't build permanent peace-loving families, with sex and close personal relations going for us, how can we ever build peace-loving nations? *The family is the revolutionary building unit,* the cell or chromosome, naturally indicated by our biological roots.

Both for individual fulfilment and for a new society, people need to hold stably together, with flying buttresses in the past to brace them against the winds of faddism and violence. When anger invades a marriage with its billy club and Mace, people must decide whether there was a permanent relation. But even if we decide we must transplant once again, we should be clear we've postponed the long-term schedule of setting down roots.

It was a natural mistake for the young people to assume that the locked box of scorpions, the hypocrisy of adult society, discredited the hope of permanence in human relations. But discovering how badly the suburb has failed should just produce the determination to do better. The one best way for the revolution to show its seriousness is in giving its elders an example of fidelity to a sick lover, a buddy in jail, a neurotic husband.

The Revelation of Sexuality in History

Human freedom was invented through the discovery of the human body under the Mediterranean sun after millennia of sculpture which showed kings, priests, gods in their rigid hieratic dress. Xenophon says again you could tell his men from the barbarians by the fact that Hellenes were brown and Persians white. Athletics at Olympia or Sparta was a segregated Garden of Eden. The sculpture is echoed by Pindar's praise of the victor in the games, celebrating a struggle against dark powers, but without inherent tragedy. Sexuality is projected onto a new understanding of the gods in the *Song* of Solomon, and when Hesiod chronicles the descent of Titanic beings from the amour of Earth with Sky.

Sexuality was no sooner liberated than corrupted, and innocence became a child's monopoly—even so with an undertow of desire and aggression. The bronze maidens on the blinding sands of Mykonos can't achieve full lack of shame, entire nakedness. Plato, who gave sexuality its place in Being, distresses us by making it not merely sublimated but homosexual, following the fashion of his times.

So the love of Achilles and Patroclus, once no different from that of David and Jonathan, "surpassing the love of women," later was given overt coloration.

The fresh start discovered by Jesus liberates all psychic powers, beginning with sexuality. Besides the political revolutionaries whose movement he co-opted for non-violence, his earliest companions were women of the street, whom he saw as closest to naturalization in the new City. Once they had been the ministrants of temple-hospitality. Before the appointment of a resident consul from his city, the travelling merchant had no protection under law except the guest-friendship of a god in his privileged sanctuary. So the temple was the first hotel, and hence the scene of what is misleadingly called "sacred prostitution." It was good business, and a religious duty, for the girls of the city like an Eskimo's daughter to provide the stranger with home comforts. By the time of Jesus, their clients were overseas mercenaries, and the old civic hospitality was no more. Somehow he restored their trust in humankind and rechanneled sexuality. Susan Sontag records that the Vietnamese rehabilitated the prostitutes of Hanoi by pampering them in country-houses and reading them fairy-tales.

The natural acceptance of sexuality by Jesus becomes strained and ambiguous in Paul, who can hold only elements in isolation: the praise of Christian love (*agapē*); the naked athlete of the Isthmian games, "I have fought the good fight, I have finished my course." Literature denatures the violence of history by naive sexual motives, deriving great events from the curiosity of an Eve, the ambition of a mythical Dido or actual Cleopatra. Pasternak organizes our experience of revolutionary change by successive liaisons: a wife from the old regime, a mistress from the new, a pickup from disintegration.

Western history is worked out in the fluctuations of sexuality: the invention of romantic love in Provence; its polarization into Puritan repression and Latin *machismo;* its projection onto the Romantic landscape. When Deism drove the old Calvinism out of Boston, it was pushed back into New Hampshire and Vermont, where it festered into our spectacular sexual deviations: polygamous Joseph Smith, Mary Baker Eddy's metaphysical prudery, chaste Transcendentalism, the segregated Shakers, the peculiar Oneida community. Long before the Wright brothers, Goethe made Faust dream of flying towards the sunset in an eternal evening over the world's seashores. The peoples of the earth play and swim at the edge of the waters they had once come out from, divested of the skins and fabrics they had picked up on dry land:

> And see the children sport upon the shore
> And hear the mighty waters rolling evermore.

Population Planning and Individual Fulfilment

It's wrong to make a woman bear six children unless she's physically very fit and her husband well-to-do:

> Oh your daddy's rich
> And your ma is good-looking.

In any case it's too many for the planet. And high birth-rate plus high infant mortality, as in India and Latin America, destroys human dignity. The poor man is forced into this ill-judged claim to esteem above all through colonialism, now inherited by America, which increased his hopes and decreased his opportunities. The high birthrate in refugee camps shows what people do when they haven't got anything to do; the whole world is becoming a refugee camp from vanished community.

A crash program of population control is a temporary necessity:

> There was an old woman who lived in a shoe.
> She had so many children!
> (She didn't know what to do.)

But in the end nothing will do but an economic system where people can see more than a marginal standard of living when they limit their families. If American investment is too paternalistic to allow this, local nationalisms must arise, presumably socialist, perhaps not too closely tied to Russia or China.

The human being can live in the arctics or tropics, devise means of survival in the depths of the sea or outer space. But the efflorescence of culture—with all its ambiguities—came from temperate climates. We'll do well not to push our plasticity too far. Especially the facts of being female put limits on the adaptability of the species. An element of woman's liberation is her recognition that she's one check to complete male destruction of the globe.

The interruption of a physical cycle produces general frustration. Jet flight over several time zones distorts the organism for a day or so, and diplomats or businessmen aren't supposed to negotiate immediately upon arrival. Childbirth is an integral part of the woman's sexual cycle. Her excitation rises and falls more slowly than the man's, and is less localized. She's not quite released from tension until nursing brings on the uterine contractions which snap the rubber band back to nearly where it was before. How to reconcile family planning with release from tension? America has settled on the contraceptive pill as the basic means of planning, and others than doctors need to discuss the problems it creates.

Spokesmen for the sexual revolution point to the "separation of sexuality from conception" as a biological fact. How far is it a psychological fact? The pill, although it accentuates the lunar cycle, in other respects gives the impression of being pregnant. When girls first start it, a number report dizziness and trouble in focussing—effects much more widespread than scattered reports of blood-clotting. Some get prematurely broad in the hips—perhaps not just with the better eating which comes from cooking for a man, but also with cumulative pseudo-pregnancy. Others feel the pill is trippy, they're walking drugstores, turning themselves on and off, up and down.

Cautious women have a lively suspicion of the untested chemicals of the drug business, remembering thalidomide. For better or worse, in or out of marriage, some have gone on with mechanical or chemical contraception, accepting as a lesser evil the psychic barrier from its being awkward, messy, not fully reliable. In general we shouldn't expect to find a way of cutting ourselves off completely from the biological conditions of our existence.

For a different reason—the daily schedule required—the pill doesn't work in illiterate village societies. Underdeveloped countries doing population control are better off with the Loop, which doesn't require maintenance and is less likely to have unknown long-term effects. While individually not foolproof, it works well statistically; that's fine so long as the villagers are willing to be treated as statistics.

We must firmly squash down the part of us that still hankers back to frontier America, when big families were an economic asset on farms of indefinite acreage. One branch of medicine we can certainly cut back on is helping childless couples to have babies—especially when the remedy may bring multiple births. Rather we should treat their sterility as a precious natural resource, and help them turn it to good use. Here may be the means to take the pressure of guilt off the homosexual.

The urgency of having fewer people points to abortion in more cases than now legal, above all when a deformed child is likely. We must just live with the damage it does to the woman's body and psyche. Of course, repressive laws (as with abortion and marijuana) are one of the roadblocks by which the American system in its folly detours reform into revolution. We might meditate on the fact that Greeks and Romans, the inventors of human dignity, exposed a deformed child at birth, before the father had acknowledged it as a person with legal rights. This unsentimental realism about the requirements of a hard world sprang from reluctance to clutter up the earth with nonviable beings. Still we've decided that this is an improper decision for any person to make; all the more then we should take extra pains not to overstep our prerogatives elsewhere.

A Family Schedule

Moralists have little business to sit around and criticize the courting practices of a society; much business to criticize a society which forces courting practices on young people many years before the desirable time to have children. Where moderate delay of awakening does no damage, our current premature sexualization deprives people of the privilege of having been children, and gets them married too young. The Vietnamese, admired by American revolutionaries, although their strength lies in past fertility, prescribe three delays to their young women: if they fall in love, to delay engagement; if they get engaged, to delay marriage; if they get married, to delay having children. Sexual liberation is seen as a barrier to vocational liberation. If we find these antiseptic heroines unattractive, we have the burden of working out something better.

It's damaging for a couple to use any means of contraception for an extended period of years at the beginning of their relationship. Having no children or even one child doesn't give enough reason to be living together—which always creates more problems than it solves. And an unmarried couple needs a double commitment to hold together.

A lot of the girls show another symptom of pseudo-pregnancy: irrational short temper. A girl living childless with a man, whether married or unmarried, wavers between fears of losing him if she gets sick or fired, and threats of leaving him. Behind fear and threat lies the growing boredom of continued sexuality with the same person which never leads to the creation of anything—except endless work on a Ph.D. thesis, or savings for a second car for her to get a better job to earn money to save for a better second car . . . And in any case the lingering fear (or hope) of unplanned pregnancy. The pseudo-pregnancy of the pill bears more of the disadvantages of the real thing than we realize—and none of the advantages.

The other side of the fertility dilemma appears when couples marry early, get the right-size family by the middle twenties, and then have to face twenty years of contraception at the other end. Not all children want to be pals with parents no older than great big brothers and sisters. We need once again a *normal schedule* of marriage (if only as a pattern to deviate from) which will minimize frustrations. So much is now known in scholarship, the sciences, the professions, that professional training for both men and women should extend into the late twenties. A married person with children usually makes it through graduate school with competent work, but without the imagination and depth ideally required.

If people get married in the late twenties, they can further utilize the natural cycle of the woman's recuperation, which makes it easier to have children about three years apart. Children closer together tire out the mother and compete for attention on the same level. In this way childbearing can end in the late thirties, when it's less desirable for both mother and baby. Then there isn't a long period of contraception ahead. Also the demands of the children and one or two professional careers channel energy away from sexuality.

A new spontaneous sentiment for planning is the trend for couples to have one or two children of their own and then adopt multiracial orphans from at home or abroad. It maximizes benefits from genetic intermixture, liberal training, the cheerful solidarity of big families. The extra care required for adopted babies also helps take pressure off sexuality. (But of course a properly functioning world wouldn't produce all those babies to be put out for adoption.)

For the mother, childbirth and lactation are the end of a cycle; for the child, a beginning. It's preferable for him to go ahead from it with a permanent father and mother—in accordance with the facts of his conception, which he somehow understands even before it's explained in the learning context of the playground. Children brought up otherwise have something left out of their makeup, which can be compensated but not replaced by a different kind of intensity.

To acquiesce in the constant breakup of radical families and liaisons as a revolutionary necessity, even when spending time in separate jails, is a counsel of despair. The anarchist theory of loosing indiscriminate sexuality onto society disrupts the movement for change as much as it does the System. Not merely pressure of vocational training, but also the risky work which only the young can do, point strongly to postponement of marriage. Student revolutionaries approaching the magic age of thirty are now moving into stable marriages. They don't need to breed big families themselves, since they're converting a new generation of middle-class rebels—themselves often products of a liberal happy suburban fortress.

Within a repressive society in rapid change, the personnel of the revolution can always be recruited from the decaying order of things. Hence a myth of the world's end, where having children is secondary. The full force of personality, so seldom realized, can be channelled into organizing. Paul sees so big a burden of interpretation on persons like himself as to rule out marriage—which in the Roman world had broken down much more completely than in ours, and had to be rebuilt precisely on the basis of the new community. John Wesley in the face of unevangelized Europe and America saw it imperative for the herald to spend a number of years unmarried.

The archaic discipline of the Catholic Church plays an ambiguous role. On one hand, its intransigence on birth control and clerical marriage, its complicated pretenses about divorce and childrearing, make people unable to see it as an actual guide for faith or morals. On the other hand, its members who voluntarily took on celibacy exhibit a spirituality of population control, and form a revolutionary vanguard, unfettered to vote for the future in a time of cosmic troubles. These inner contradictions will only be resolved through an infusion of Protestant liberty in new-style reunion.

The mistakes venial for individuals are mortal for societies. Paul's harsh words about sexual deviation in the early chapters of *Romans* are sociological analysis; family breakdown is an index of social collapse. The very fact that it's easy and forgivable for individuals to go wrong implies something unforgivable about society. *Our* moralists can't find words harsh enough for our Madison Avenue temples of prostitution.

The Family as Unit of Rebuilding

The New Testament sees the solidarity in the local community as its marriage to Christ. Today the solidarity of the Church is fractured into denominations. If people are well-informed enough to know they want something claimed by one of the denominations—a liturgy, a system of discipline—they also know it doesn't say what they must hear. A spirituality of marriage adequate to the situation cuts across existing divisions.

In the marriage vows, the fresh start of baptism into nonviolence must be channelled into an undertaking not to overburden the planet, the oppressed, the partner. Likewise through the mysterious process of education people must help their children to make the same choice as they did, but no less freely. Actual sensitivity about personal relations is almost as hard to achieve in a house as on a planet. If we can reach across the earthquake-fault here, we can hope to reach across it anywhere. And it *has* been bridged here from time to time. If a peacemaker isn't determined on actual integrity with wife or husband, we don't have to take that peacefulness very seriously anywhere else.

Revolutionary movements at one stage must be Puritanical. How can a vacation, a place by the sea, guestrooms and a garden, violin lessons be squared with the austerity and urgency of the present? But these are the things we're fighting for, and they must be built somehow into the revolution, or they won't be there when it succeeds. One of the places where the old violence is first overcome is in a family of Bachs, Huxleys, Wesleys. Even a whole community of Quakers can build a new constructive life on the rubble of the old society.

Both suburban and revolutionary families shipwreck on the transformation of sexuality. In a certain year, there seems to be nothing holding husband and wife together but a bunch of fractious children. Still, the widening gap needn't be anybody's fault or even something wrong. The original job is starting to be wound up; the children are taking their life into their own hands, more independent than anybody gave them credit for. "Daddy, us third-graders had a sitdown today. We sat down outside the classroom for half an hour. We demanded no more substitutes."

At this point the parents' cue is to keep on switching creativity to the task which both they and the children can recognize as above all legitimate. *No more substitutes.* Perhaps a deepening involvement of the woman in what the man is doing. But the very notion of a profession in which the wife can take legitimate interest and pride shows how far we've got to move from the current job scene. Much more, for husband and wife to work out an actual joint project. Whatever woman's liberation means for them, both must radically rethink the channelling of creativity. How can it find a profession which will support the family and still express their rock-bottom convictions as it blossoms into usefulness?

chapter SIX

The Demand for Usefulness: Actual Vocation

The need for food, and aggression with its complex roots, push man into his daily work. But our "economic" system isn't any longer what its name implies, a rational "household management" of the planet. Its jobs fit neither into intelligible long-range goals nor individual fulfilment. There they sit, rootless parasites in the jungle of competition (itself rooted in no proper soil but its own decay), bearing ostentatious purple flowers untouched by sun, wind, and rain.

The Crisis of Counter-Productive Jobs

Jacques Ellul has analyzed with pitiless logic how the growth of knowledge has forced all jobs, and the society which they allegedly serve, into a cycle of self-expanding *technique*, recognizing no principles but itself, doing whatever can be done because it can be. If the supply of raw materials were infinite, what ever could break the cycle? Our finitude is our salvation. The limitations of planetary ecology, of the poor's patience, of our inner balance, ensure that at some point technique will destroy the conditions for its own existence. We could still hope to smash its handcuffs a little before the whole environment spontaneously breaks down. The most important sciences are the ones which laid out the groundplan of natural orders before they were stifled by the fungus growth of technique: ecology, Marxist historical analysis, the classical literatures which define individual freedom.

John Calvin, who wound up the clock of our economic system by inventing the delayed gratification of saving, left the goals and means of the professions inadequately examined. To the industrial and imperial West he gave the dogma that any job which actually exists has a prescriptive right to be called the service of God. The mystique of secularism ends up in the same bind; any movement which involves large numbers of people must be a proper part of the human enterprise. But we must rather ask of every job and profession whether it serves a legitimate need; and in a legitimate way, without breaking of orders. We do this by holding the System more seriously than it does itself to its self-professed principles.

What is called a "student" movement leads the push into the future, wavering between withdrawal and violence. But in either case studying is abandoned; the young people are too itchy to embark on any seven-year course of study, medicine or physics. The bridge which normally leads from curiosity to vocation loses its abutments on both ends and falls into the river.

Simultaneously the attractive power of the professions is corrupted. The scientist lets his research be chan-

nelled by grants from foundations dipping into a Defense
Department well. Businessmen acquiesce in buying personal affluence at the cost of personal stifling, and the clos-
ing of doors for billions around the world. A parasitic system of middlemen muscles in on writing and artistic
production, making and breaking fads by marketing rules,
as *Time* invented the Death of God in 1966.

Unionized labor is there serving its two collusive masters; what their hands have made is taken from them,
nothing to show their families except calluses and the pay-
check to live in the suburbs and watch the TV and stand
in line at popular restaurants. None has a second string to
his bow; even this unsatisfactory life is lived only by kind
permission of the System.

And then the young people see their professors cutting classes to get consulting fees for tightening the System's bolts. There isn't any sense of working together at a
joint task. A depression might turn people back to necessities, but is unlikely so long as the State goes on subsidizing
a military machine, and patching up inflation through
old-age benefits.

In a poor society, alienation is controlled by a class
of exploiting rich, hidden behind bureaucracy. In an
affluent society, alienation is built into the institutional
complex of the system, which generates warped parallels
to the institutions of a normally functioning society.
Under this constant pressure the whole body of the State
degenerates into a cancer feeding on itself. The media are
its pseudo-language, spreading the lie that the interests of
the technological complex are supreme. Its jobs are a manipulation of paper and men. Through it, the industrial
complex (more and more automated) turns out self-

producing instruments of destruction, self-destructing consumer products, regardless of need. Obliteration and obsolescence—a system whose humanitarian triumph is military items obsolete before used, or scrubbed on the assembly line after billions have been spent. Its foreign policy is the degradation or development of poor peoples through its diplomatic, military, industrial, academic arms. Its churches are the churches.

What makes the System seem so unapproachable is that so many people are spending their full working time (with however bad a conscience) at jobs which support it. The new things which critically need to be done involve a radical break with existing job-slots. Of course those slots are a big break with what they were a quarter-century ago, as the System progressively deforms the jobs inside itself. The aggressive retool themselves for new niches, others fall by the way.

At first, the people moving out or moving over will only seem like scattered individuals. But somewhere sometime there will be a breakthrough—beginning in the Black Caucus of many professions now. The University rebellion is serving notice that young people will not put their bodies behind the existing desks next to the potted philodendron and the glassbrick walls. With much inefficiency and waste, because of their inadequate training, they're groping for new slots to move into. But also the vanguard of the professionals—those with exceptional political consciousness or professional competence—are beginning to make the break. Physicists and physicians are taking the Hippocratic oath of revolutionary humanism not to lend themselves to the System's purposes of war and intimidation.

The Revolution of Inner Discipline

The new consciousness of vocation began when professionals discovered that, while the unions slept behind them, they were in the vanguard by virtue of condemning the settled foreign policy of their Government *on their own principles.* When doctors denounced it for maiming civilians; anthropologists as genocidal; biologists as destroying a unique environment; statesmen as imprudent; lawyers as illegal; ambassadors as bad public relations; clergy as immoral—the Government could only set up its last smoke screens to persuade its captive generals not to condemn it as bad tactics, or its economists as bad investment.

We can tell that the System is set on pulling itself down when its own logic again and again reminds us of its final refutation—our ineradicable dissatisfaction. I just got a questionnaire for my twenty-fifth reunion yearbook. Was I on schedule? Were any of my children hippies? Were they attending the old school? How did I estimate my net worth? Was my portfolio for income or growth? What was my house valued at? Over against seniority, tenure, and investments, the principal hope for the future is our dynamic security of getting fired to do the next thing on the agenda of the cosmos. You may thumb your nose at your boss: "Something is happening here, and you don't know what it is, do you, Mr Jones?" *It's the finger of God writing out new job-descriptions.*

Past needs have produced specialized forms of personal discipline—the monk, the missionary, the inventor, the entrepreneur. We ask for an American da Vinci to diagram the proportions of a man. People do all that drinking, watching ball games on TV, golf, driving around on the freeways, because they can't face spending time on themselves. From the lack of any gravitational mass in those empty lives, by an exact law the high-velocity children spin off centrifugally into new eccentric orbits.

A man becomes himself by what he does: "In the beginning was the *deed*." The self-affirmation of a fresh start, the creativity which temporarily flowed into the pool of sexuality, are supposed in the end to fill up the ocean of a "vocation," something you're called to by the nature of things. Our co-workers there are built up with us into a professional team. How can it pass from being the arena of competition, where men are ground down into identical grains of sand, to a nuclear cell of actual community?

Craftsmanship as Affirmation of Natural Orders

Our demand for usefulness is another form of the cry for meaning. Our community began to cohere for the first time while we wrapped hundreds of pounds of donated pennies to bail out our brothers and sisters in jail. In our need for perfection, our own spoiled craftsmanship throws us back on the primordial creativity. We find our meaning in work—and not just anything which calls itself work, but the work of the revolutions of peace, done in solidarity with that archaic revolution which once lifted the cosmos up bright and dripping out of the seismic waves of chaos.

After the initial procreative act of creation, our tradition sees its nuts-and-bolts detail as the work of a master tinker who hammers the earth out flat, and the sky as an Achilles' shield. "The sky announces the splendor of God, and the firmament shows the work of his hands" (Ps. 19:2). Before that burst of creativity all is waste and void —there's no proper light, no birds in the air, all subject to earthquake. Then the architect sets up the seven pillars supporting the circular temple of the universe, and so stabilizes all.

As we walk through the forest, by an act of concentration we can focus on the billions of atoms in a leaf, and then think out to the waves of the sea, trying to grasp the extent of the matter in all the planets and galaxies. It's full of mysteries. Where are all the negative protons which should have been formed to balance off the positive ones in our part of the universe? Do the galaxies alternate matter and anti-matter? Anyway, wherever we look, everything is full of organization; somebody has been hard at work.

Our task is patiently to extricate the horse imprisoned in the jade, the cherries latent under the bark, the potential man overlaid by the frightened bully. In our part of the creation the most important things are human beings and the forms they define themselves in—words. The literary scholar instructed in the area of liberation brings out of his safe-deposit box new things and old things. Since *we* can't add an inch to our height, our work doesn't consist in making new things but in remaking existing ones, polishing tarnished silver. The master we're all apprenticed to did *his* apprenticeship in the living grain of wood or stone, and then graduated as community-organizer and poet.

Excellence: Beating the System
at Its Own Game

If the military is our profession we need to switch. But if we have a potentially rational vocation, our cue is neither to drop out, nor to lose hope, nor to go on climbing the ladder in hopes of gradual change; but to *beat the System at its own game.* If we take seriously the professed principles of business, the Church, law, engineering, foreign policy, medicine, we'll find that they sit in judgment on the System and condemn large areas of current practice. If we try to drop out, someday we'll have to drop back in again into compromise with the System— an unfruitful one, because we haven't got the competence to attack it head-on. After initial rebellion, a student should learn his profession exceptionally well, get his credentials, and then turn his back on its promise of security. Swamp the profession with the reality of your work, and then use that bridgehead to push its compromised goals through to the universal goals they imply.

Of course our contracts will frequently be terminated. We must keep firmly in mind that we're the ones who've been entrusted with the true principles of the System, and that *it knows it.* It hopes we'll crawl back humbled. But if we bounce back with double energy and even more extensive proposals, better credentials than ever, it can't exclude us from the discussion. Because the apparently reliable are more or less phony careerists, who at graduate school every time cut the lectures on professional ethics. In the end it's not the threat from the System that holds us back, but our slothful self-destructive suspicion that the System may be right. Push beyond that; everything salvageable in the System will be salvaged only because able men not easily hurt have kept holding it up to its word.

Every harlot was a virgin once, every bureaucrat was at one time a man, and we do him the credit of calling him back to himself. Of course we may not bring over the top management *en bloc*. They are at this very moment pretending that automation or group-dynamics is allowing the System to break through its old ways and become radically responsive to our wishes—if we'll only be patient. But our patience has lasted five thousand years and things aren't all that different.

Let it not offer us the cookies of minor concessions, or manipulate us by alternating patronage and neglect. We stick with it because we don't set ourselves up as founders of a counter-System; we propose to keep our lines open to the radicals of the next generation, who will be born inside *it*. We're stuck with the System as we're stuck with the planet; we have to retain confidence that renewal is possible within both. If we hold a true measure of the depth of its problems, we won't be fobbed off by its usual alternation of cynicism and complacency.

We will deal with the System on our scale, not its. It's as impossible to reconstruct a whole economic system as a whole continental biology; it operates by uncounted big and little mechanisms which slip through the meshes of every planner. What we can hope to do is: to halt by political action the major operations which are destroying natural orders; to introduce correct principles in small areas where we more nearly have control; and then patiently to observe the reaction to this preliminary injection of order. After we've shaken the aphids off the rose bush, cut down the jungle of weeds, pruned off the deadwood, watered and fertilized, we just have to wait and see where the new growth appears. It knows better than we do.

We must envisage a radical *reordering of priorities* in the professions, which can only be done by each individual in his own job and caucus. Catholic natural-law theory is a timid approach to what is needed. What Paul Goodman writes can always be read with profit. But everybody knows his own area best. We have to introduce the new genetic strains of love where we're actually operating—in the soil of the planet.

THE NATURAL ORDERS. Lawyers must find where existing legal systems are most vulnerable to an application of justice, and push them to define new principles of international law, new rights for people and things. We must encourage and fund the new breed of physicist and biologist who act as our watchdogs against the constant dangers of nuclear technology, insecticides, untried drugs, synthetic additives, substitute consumer products. We need educated farmers and ranchers who incorporate wildlife preserves on their land, observe it with love, collaborate on equal terms with professional scientists—for knowledge, not manipulation.

THE PLANET AND THE LOCAL COMMUNITY. Planners today are operating on the wrong scales: too big to be responsive to local needs, too small to be responsive to planetary needs. We must focus on each and distinguish them sharply.

Decentralizing. It must be possible for a radical banker to find a means to help the ghetto or a poor nation finance itself and then *keep his hands off*. Or for doctors to invent a bridge between lucrative private specialty and immense clinics—a modest friendly neighborhood medicine. Engineers who don't scale up but down, finding ways to reduce the need for their own work, making it invisible. City planning—better, finding a smaller level of organization without the waste of commuting, everybody bringing his specialty into a more intimate approachable scale. Dispersing industry into the fields—as Hanoi did under pressure of bombing. Local co-ops, bail bondsmen. Every step is in the right direction which destroys some possibility of national advertising.

Internationalizing. A crash program to expand the study of Russian and Chinese, as well as minor languages; developing the wisdom of the body to be at home in different climates. Lobbying to create UN conservation and rights commissions with real teeth in them. Embodying war-crimes precedents like Nuremberg and Stockholm in authoritative legal textbooks and live institutions. Using overseas loans for actual indigenous development. Genuine adaptation of Western medicine to other environments, a coordinated attack on overpopulation by different techniques. Above all, every professional on all levels saying No to the flow of war materiel and personnel.

SELF-ESTEEM AND ESTEEM FOR OTHERS. Every administrator I know is squeezed by the dilemma of having sacrificed his own creativity in favor of service to others— which turns out nonexistent. Much greater realism about both is required.

Radical service. Reliable subsidies for militant lawyers who defend the defenseless—not for a year or two as public defender (a legal chaplaincy) but lifelong. Social service that doesn't exhaust the worker or demean the receiver—because it's done to strengthen the necessary revolutions. Medical committees for human rights which take on the police as a major health problem. Above all creating the *reality* that the administrator is the servant of the creative people around him. Not accepting complex decision-making bodies, just because they're expensive and succeeded in putting a missile-bearing submarine in the water.

Humanizing. Restoring the link between workman and consumer. Contractors who will build more houses and more durable ones—with rooms for old people in them. Doctors who give a sick person *more* civilized treatment than a dinner guest. People's historians, like Staughton Lynd writing a history of the American Resistance. Teaching the right books and encouraging people to produce more of the same. Restoring a philosophical discipline which doesn't confine itself to an ingrown set of topics.

Besides the practical vocations through which the world's work is done, some must devote themselves wholly to what we all do in part: through ideology, meditation defining the meaning of the world's work. On a globe only too well explored and grown familiar, is there still a vocation for the hermit? Thomas Merton found a way in Kentucky; the Port Chicago vigil for eight hundred days witnessed to nonviolence over against napalm in darkest California.

Woman's job just as it is in most ways offers the ideal

example. Somebody who keeps the house clean, takes care of the kids, plants a vegetable garden, fixes meals, and does the laundry has carried through her share of the bargain—really, the job assigned to Adam in the management of the garden. In comparison, what's all this destruction and busywork that men are doing? The liberation of women consists in their awareness of forming the *vanguard of the green revolution.*

Not the worst but the best men today are crippled by inhibitions about putting their true impulses into action. We must remind ourselves of the enormous energies available to society—Athens, Florence, London, the frontier, the Russian revolution, the space program. And these were pagan renaissance programs, in large part exploitative, asserting power. Much deeper potential was tapped by the renewers of the Church—Francis, Luther, Fox, Wesley—carrying their vision of integrity through to its simple logical end. We have a job even more critical than theirs, we're proceeding less blindly. Why is the cry for humanization of world society no stronger? Because we don't trust the Spirit of humanity enough to make it stronger. We take a step forward and then half-draw it back, looking up and down the line to see if anybody else has taken the step; they are looking too.

But the course of events is currently issuing the *command* to march. Perhaps radical renewal won't come until our preliminary commitment to family or career is destroyed by persecution. Honest Frenchmen could unite against their country's Algerian policy—so much more humane than *our* colonialism—because facile hopes had already been shattered in the Resistance of World War II. Its members—Camus, Ellul—could return to normal life and a career of deepened insight, but only because they'd once given up the certainty of those things. In America, students and the young haven't yet reached that desperation; only the blacks as yet can place their hope in having given up hope.

Restoration of Working Community in the Church

Hebrew literature, like early Greek literature, is both science and history in embryo. By reading those texts against our current understanding of nature and society, we come to see the unavoidable conditions of our existence here. The New Testament alone defines what it means to be a free individual, rooted in the natural and social environments but transcending them. Each man, as his own priest in his own vocation, has to work out those insights concretely for himself. By cooperative effort we do the jobs called for by the revolution.

Most vocations don't carry their final meaning in themselves. The farmer, businessman, workman produce things to sustain life; the doctor, social worker maintain it against threats. For what purpose? The actual meaning of life lies in the symbolic forms which define it. The poet is called the maker *par excellence*. The poetry behind us says that a plastic force beyond matter and energy calls things into being by a *word*. The act of naming—self-definition, celebrating—is what the others exist for, the principal employment of Eden.

Language, the word, is the business of us all. The spirit or breath of wisdom that all our works should be done in finds its primary task in speaking the word which guides all the others. Literature is the center of education; it's the light which makes the trades, arts, sciences, professions transparent of humanity.

In the new community building up around us, each man from his own learning and experience helps formulate goals for himself and others. Our solidarity in what we call the Church is our confidence that others, drawing from the same wells, have the same trust in us as we in them. Without the need of interminable conferences, by our built-in unity of goal we're workers on one team.

Most of our errors are ignorance; we manage to overlook the record which shows other people in textbook fashion falling into the trap which lies in front of us. The statesman, whether Establishment or revolutionary, can only operate by manipulation of men and movements. The real revolution happens when poets are the *acknowledged* legislators of mankind. Not a Vergil but an Augustus builds an oppressive empire; not an Archbishop but a Fox builds a new community. As we pass through our apprenticeship we come face to face with power, the heart of the dark forces, and we realize we can't beat *it* at its own game of coercion. We can only help people get organized through the powerlessness of the word. The legions of Beelzebub are supreme in their own non-realm; the chains by which they've bound mankind don't fall except by the folly of preaching. Community is only built through the unconditional demand for justice, which in the end goes beyond all politics.

chapter SEVEN

The Demand for Justice: Going Beyond Power

So far as individuals or families trust each other, they're organized by voluntary agreement into community. So far as they don't, they're organized by coercion into the State; a majority or large minority is oppressed. The first step towards community is the demand to restore justice for the oppressed. Since trust and distrust will continue, our organization will contain elements of both coercion and freedom. Of course they don't stand on the same level, and some adjustments between them are more desirable than others.

The Impotence and Danger of Power

Coercion is a more pervasive element of our world than choice; but we can't be so clear that it's actually exercised *by* somebody. The agents of coercion do what they do because *they're* told to by their superiors, or by the tradition of their fellows. The head of the department has to reckon with those traditions; with the politicians who shield certain interests; with influential pressure-groups.

Coercion isn't willed by one man and can't be altered by one man; it's just there, like the law of gravity. Its first victim is the man who thinks he exercises it.

An individual works himself up in the hierarchy of coercion by following certain rules: recognition of his powerlessness to change things, willingness to go along with the system. You can't speak about a moral or immoral man in this context, but only about a strong or weak man. The strong man is consistent about responding to pressures from various directions, and so gravitates into top positions. The weak man wobbles—maybe he's just stupid. Society gets precisely the police and administrators it bargains for, who respond like a seismograph to minute shifts of mass. If a man wants to reform the police, chief of police is the last office he should run for.

The President of the United States is essentially powerless. Robert Kennedy's account of the Cuban missile crisis shows the impotence of his brother and Khrushchev, going through foreordained military and diplomatic rituals. We do want a strong man as President, to register accurately the pressures acting on him without cracking, so that we have something to rely on. If he gets imprisoned by the military and Intelligence, or by his party, the system becomes unstable through the automatic reaction of the slighted groups. But the individual voter can't do anything even to get the strong man in. Any other aims of a man besides ambition in running for President are irrelevant. Kennedy, Johnson, Nixon, very different in style, were all ruthless, industrious, ambitious—and powerless. The war, the deterioration of the cities, space exploration ran their apparently destined courses, independent of these men's policies—or lack of them.

As you go further down the ladder to a Congressman

or administrative appointee, some offices permit true elements of choice and influence on policy: being a watchdog
of civil rights, an advocate of reform. On this level political pressures are only partial; provided the man satisfies
his constituents in certain areas, he's free to be himself in
others. But just because he'd like to end a war, patch up
the city, dismantle the missiles, doesn't mean he can do it.
Not much change will be accomplished through Congress-
men whose constituencies (and therefore their own views)
differ only fractionally from the ruling elite. The biggest
potentially deviant constituencies here are of blacks, perhaps youth—certainly not yet women. It would be wildly
unrealistic to think of running for Congress as a sheep in
wolf's clothing. The most hopeful politics is a straight-out
radical campaign. But the biggest influences for change in
the sixties came from quite outside the constitutional
scheme.

The growth of technology as communications gave
the poor a new knowledge of their own strength; as
affluence, it gave them hopes it's impossible to deny. Establishment political theory lays it down as dogma that the
biggest threat is always from anarchic forces of disorder—
Vikings, Turks, bikies, militants, hippies, Commies. Its
claimed first concern is to legitimate a central authority
which can impose law and order. Only then will it appeal
to the morality or interests of the rulers to mitigate their
use of authority.

In older times, the damage which could be done by
any leader of men, however charismatic and perverse, was
limited; both nature and society absorbed all the blows he
could give it. Bubonic plague was a greater threat. Today
in a number of countries, offices staffed by robot bureau-
crats hold the power to damage permanently the whole

planetary living system. What we have to fear isn't the raw power of anarchic rootless masses, but those rationalizing technical procedures, operating through impersonal institutions, which have replaced all personal centers of authority.

Oppressed groups hardly anywhere threaten to take over the governing system as such, but only to amputate its illegitimate extensions, the pseudopods of the world-amoeba. Still the System cynically creates the fear that if power is taken from the hands of the moderate humane civilized men who now exercise it, after a period of anarchy it will fall to unbalanced passionate militants who will impose a reign of terror. A second Hitler—this time with nuclear weapons at his disposal. Of course, something worse than the present can always be imagined. But the time to cry out against murder, the place where we need to be most on guard against Hitlerism, is never the future but the *present*.

Russia is a threat to world community today, not because she's undergone a revolution, but because she *hasn't*, she continues Czarist oppression in industrial format. America is a threat, not because she represents something new but something old: European racist imperialism with different techniques. If China becomes a serious threat, it will be because in her externally imposed isolation she couldn't break the habit of bureaucracy.

Our Provisional Commitment to Politics

Our commitment to any political goals must always be provisional. For the goals will be partial, with their own element of injustice; also they will be further compromised in the process of moving towards them. That doesn't mean we shouldn't be committed. Before any global action for conservation, before any step to inner integrity, must first come our response to the demand for justice. Working for justice is so critical a problem precisely because we're not sure how to go about it. But we'd better not let that doubt paralyze us into a twin of the complacency which pretends there isn't any problem. Better a provisional passionate commitment to a political failure than no commitment. The means of our politics may appear nonpolitical; but the ends must always be revolutionary, recognizing each injustice, old and new, and overthrowing it as fast as possible.

Precisely as a result of our adherence, the formerly oppressed group may gain real power. Since we're all of one nature, that group will have the same temptation as its predecessors: using its new power to oppress other groups in turn. Since every growth has its roots, its misuse of power springs from the very beginnings of the revolutionary struggle, however disinterested or quixotic its cause then seemed.

Other commitments are directed towards a permanent human or natural object—a wife, a forest, a body of learning. But our commitment to justice can never take any political institution for granted. The corruption of politics makes politics the *most religious of occupations,* where it's necessary always to have in mind a transcendent object with no adequate representation in history. Beyond every application of justice here, we're pushed back to an overriding principle of justice which by the facts of the case can't be embodied in any human institution.

Any particular legal system deserves our provisional

assent as an effort to embody justice on one level. But the sanction of any legal system is coercion; it will always be used by the class in power to strengthen itself and put down any possible competitors. Our partial assent to the law of man also forces us beyond it into an absolute assent to what may be called the law of God.

Augustine asked if it was proper for a man to sit as judge and pass sentence; he gave the answer Yes. So far as I know he didn't adequately realize the corruption of the legal system in its own terms. We who do, must give a different answer. A man may sit if (1) in day-by-day decisions he can carry out substantially better justice than a less conscientious man; and (2) if he takes the sting out of his complicity with the massive injustice remaining by using the leverage of his judgeship to work for judicial reform. But for a man who has agreed this far to work with the corrupt system there can't be any vacation, any sleep.

In general, any job (say, a policeman's) within a warped structure is justifiable just so far as we can use it to start straightening the distortion. If our day-by-day work necessarily involves us in deep complicity, our usefulness for reform is destroyed in advance, we haven't got any leverage. We needn't worry about the positions falling vacant, there will always be policemen and judges. If the policeman is essentially a pawn, so that neither a kindly nor a sadistic man on the job changes the character of the work done, this is no place to waste our kindliness. For we can always choose to work for change through a vocation which isn't so fatally handicapped.

As a matter of fact, power operating through law today mostly carries out the will of a demonic System, overruling the merits of the persons who fill its positions.

An idealist is trapped where a cynic is at home. For the idealist is forced to pretend that he's acting out of principle when he's acting out of necessity. And then, instead of justifying his actions as conditional necessities of state, he justifies them as absolute necessities of morality.

When injustice is being done to a group inside the System, we can work actively to help it without attributing exclusive virtue to its claims. Liberal intellectuals rightly supported the labor movement between the two World Wars. But today, with improvement in the status of labor, the principal injustices done by the System are to groups which *don't* form part of it.

The instinctive first step towards justice is normally to exercise the limited violence for good which we were taught—except this time on behalf of the oppressed over against the Establishment. But as we reflect back on our Establishment past, we can see that both sides are the same species and will fall into the same traps. There doesn't seem to be any way now of keeping the family fight down to the old-fashioned level, which may bruise some limbs but is guaranteed not to pull the house down.

So we go on repeating to the System the warning of ancient wisdom to beware of presumptuous arrogance—with less and less confidence that our warning will be heard. Meanwhile we struggle, if necessary through that same System, towards means of control for the violence against the environment which has priced itself out of the international market, a luxury not the richest can afford. Frustrated there also, we transfer our political task to provisional support for the most hopeful revolutionary movements, and try to humanize and moderate their methods by our presence. At the same time we renew our absolute commitment to building a nonpolitical revolution of voluntary community. Jacques Ellul defines our fundamental working principle: to abandon the revolution as soon as it succeeds, and go over to the side of the new class of the oppressed.

By all signs, the United States is in for a basic change in the way it does things—a second American Revolution. Bloody or not? Blacks, hippies, students here are as deeply identified as they could be with their Vietnamese brothers and sisters. If Viet Nam is part of America, enough blood has been shed to glut any theorist of revolution.

Even in face of a likely right-wing reaction, I suppose we should be hoping and working for a change in America that would: do actual justice to blacks and other minorities; recognize student power; take over some corporate monopolies; modify the policy of intervention overseas; develop a safeguard of trust and then dismantle missile-installations; end the draft and political repression; repeal marijuana laws; control insecticides. And even those modest demands, which just begin to touch our deeper alienation, sound wildly Utopian.

But in any case white and black revolutionaries here will remain very much children of the American System. Their tactics are the realistic exercise of violence which they've been taught by the practice of their elders, or by the theology of a Reinhold Niebuhr. They will share with their forerunners the illusion that full control over one's society is possible and desirable. After the State has been replaced or changed—certainly with new pretensions, perhaps not so intractable as before—nearly all the critical jobs will remain to be completed by free persons in voluntary community.

The Transcending of Power

So long as we continue to operate solely in the political realm, we have to keep assessing greater and lesser injustice. But our study of history could still convince us, in the most pragmatic political terms, that even an apparently "just" war of liberation was an actual step towards global nuclear war. In that case its justice would become some kind of mirage in the light of ultimate expediency.

There may be a way of lessening both injustice and the likelihood of atomic war which doesn't lie along the route of politics. It would mean renouncing the effort to reconstruct society as a whole from positions of power; the current rulers of the State would be left where they are. Instead: organizing people without coercion. We have no idea how far this mode of organization could be extended, reducing the damage done by the State while letting it stay in power. Never before have the penalties of failure been so great or so obvious. By the nature of the effort, an attempt at noncoercive organization can't increase the violence-level, at worst it can only fail; at all times it's worth a try.

We shall never lack candidates for the White House or episcopal sees. The business of politicians is making compromises; we can leave that up to them, we needn't butt into their business. Our cue is to present them with the whole package, the best way we can see it, of what's required by love, by justice, by survival. The more healthy currents there are at work in our society, the better politicians we're likely to get; but it's not one of the things we can work for directly. This must be what Paul meant by saying that the ruler was appointed by God. We do our thing, and take what Providence supplies. Politics is incurably ambiguous. Definitive political affirmations apply only to the realm of our final citizenship. Paradoxically, only through that realm can the historic nations of the planet be held back from self-destruction.

A Road Not Taken: Removing the Missile-Threat

Even more ominous than the current scenes of actual violence is the double missile screen bracketing the North Pole, together with Polaris submarines and other deployments. Our military expenditures, our foreign policy are designed around the fear and threat of using those systems. If military spending were reduced, Forman's half billion could be seen for the peanuts it is. The one biggest security we could win for the planet would be the certainty that neither Russia nor America would intentionally set off their missiles. A discussion of alternatives will illustrate the possibility of transcending power. If the balance of terror were removed, the missiles could start being dismantled. They don't need to be replaced by a hundred percent foolproof system; they're not absolutely foolproof themselves.

This isn't the Utopianism of unilateral disarmament or World Federalism, but a hope which, pushed hard enough by voluntary agencies, could possibly be endorsed by atavistic governments. If anybody wants to know why so many people have given up on our leaders as criminals or fools, let him recollect that during the whole anti-ballistic-missile debate no influential voice was raised to suggest an alternative to the whole preventive lunacy.

Instead of the present system of conflicting interests, what is needed is a system of identical interests. The simplest way would be at all times to have so many Americans in Russia, and so many Russians here, that neither government could strike the other, from the certainty of the death or imprisonment of those hostages. Both sides would be much more careful not to have missiles go off accidentally, knowing their own citizens were on target. The initiative for peace which we like to claim would be preserved if we offered to fund the entire program. We would simply both send students to the other country, with return visas valid when the total of a million on each side had been built up. It would be money well spent, unlike that on missile folly. The same procedure, unlike missile-deployment, would be flexible enough for adaptation to Soviet-Chinese hostility. A fixed percent annual turnover of persons would be written in, so that neither government could write off the absentees as disloyal emigrants.

Why hasn't it been started already? Our dismay at the current technology, bureaucracy, modes of decision-making is that *they look for the wrong kind of solutions to problems*. When faced with mutual suspicion of America and Russia after World War II, neither set of planners tried to deal with it by diplomacy, movements of old-fashioned persons. Instead they used enormous amounts of brainpower to create technology which vastly increased the suspicions. Each side in its own thinking bears more responsibility, since each claims to be the open and innovative system.

The Cross as Sacrament of Power

We talk as if the dilemma between Establishment violence and revolutionary violence was a discovery of our own, to which traditional beliefs must adapt themselves and give a radically new answer. But our traditional beliefs consist precisely in the affirmation that the dilemma has already been resolved. S. G. Brandon's *Jesus and the Zealots,* a book making some splash among Christian revolutionaries, conclusively proves what should never have been doubted or forgotten, that most of Jesus' associates had long been members of a revolutionary guerrilla movement. Brandon is less successful in doing away with the unanimous evidence of the Gospels that Jesus found a different line to take; in discovering the real author of the pacifism which he has the Evangelists ascribe to Jesus; or in explaining why *this* executed Messianic claimant should have been remembered rather than another.

In fact the Gospels in the most literal way possible give the cue for our action over against both exploitation and revolution. The breaking and restoration of all the orders simultaneously are seen in an execution carried out by the imperial power: the one uniquely *free individual,* the representative of the *oppressed poor,* expected as Son of Man to restore the *biological order* of Eden. The Gospels show individuals as responsible—Caiaphas, Herod, Pilatus. Paul sees *them* in turn as agents of demonic forces ignorant of the hidden wisdom of God; "For if they had known it, they would not have executed the lord of splendor" (I Cor. 2: 18). Those Powers have infiltrated the

State so deeply that one Caesar can only be overthrown by another, and we may just as well give the Caesar we've got what belongs to him.

The new vision was the possibility of a counter-organization of society based not on coercion but voluntary adherence: the thing which Jesus has no name for but simply illustrates and builds, which Paul names the Church. Its ideology was verified through its anchor in the remotest past—its conviction that Law and Prophets pointed to the new organization. Likewise around the world today, the work of prophets and of Jesus together make up *our* lever on the past. Both then and now, the agreed-on literary text and historical event behind us generate in our scattered communities common forms of art, liturgy, polity, sexuality, direct action.

The meaning of the ancient city, which produced those texts and events, is a local pattern for planetary community. If agriculture was an enterprise conceived in the first village units of food-gatherers, the city preceded the farm, and remains the center for global management. The model can never cut itself off sharply from the surrounding territory; in every age the bearer of the future is the man who carries the new discoveries of that community into the next outer circle. Studying foreign languages is the basic symbol of our true internationalism, and it's scandalous that hardly any Americans except CIA agents know Vietnamese.

The proclamation of the Gospel—the interruption of all other programs for a special announcement that the Liberated Zone of love is at hand—affirms that no dilemmas are insoluble; we never find ourselves in a moral box. The apparent contradiction between the necessity of revolution, and the certainty that (as Jim Bevel says) murder is no revolution, just points to the reality that revolution must be somewhere else. We are supposed to beat revolutionaries at their own game—that is, to join them in their condemnation of injustice, and to see injustice also in whatever methods they've taken over from the enemy.

The Marxist theory of the withering away of the State is correct in the sense that its functions must gradually be taken over by noncoercive organizations. It's false in the sense that if the State withers away obviously, a successor State will rush into the vacuum. Our cue is to leave it there, enjoying affluence and prestige, discouraging competitors of the same sort; and simultaneously to draw its teeth, to move people from inside it effectively to another place, reducing the power of that Gulliver to trample people by tying him hand and foot with a thousand gentle threads, to confuse and disarm him with love.

The true unofficial ambassadors of the city dispense with its passports and weapons, going out on their task of organizing the next adjacent province. That control can only be exercised through the paradoxical means of non-self-assertion; in no other way will its claim to universality be generally acceptable. As soon as we push the principles of any politics through to their end, they overthrow its announced aims in favor of more inclusive ones. Unlike every other art or science, politics dissolves itself without residue and points beyond itself to another sphere. The only invincible weapon, the sacrament of politics, is the Cross; the sole ultimately viable community is the Church. The scapegoat liberator suffers in the wilderness outside the city for the city's benefit; his humiliation is the ultimate definition of politics. What has been called the death of God is the discovery that fulfilment is achieved through powerlessness.

Nonviolence as Unique Principle of Community

Because of our defects in solidarity with the oppressed, by the time we come over to their side they've already hit on a partly violent solution. Our guilt requires us to assent provisionally to their violence, as in some sense embodying justice, while still trying to mitigate it. *Their violence corresponds to our tardiness.* For where a people's cry for justice has found an adequate leader from the very beginning, he can exercise pure nonviolence. As justice to the biological environment consists in letting it be itself, so justice to our brother consists in letting him be himself.

The Church as we see it has been recast in the plastic mold of that State which to save its credibility has murdered millions of our brothers. Its current form is a web of competing assertions of ecclesiastical power, draining off the energy which should go into actual work. If we think to leave it to wither on the vine over there, it still claims a monopoly on the symbolic forms which we need to operate by. We've got to go and reclaim our inheritance by reorganizing the current heirs, however unpromising they may seem. That necessary reunion and renewal can only be effected by the Cross, in a renunciation of rival claims and of competition with the State, through a joint recognition of powerlessness.

The State, in the grip of demonic forces, is blind. Still

it senses in the Church a threat to its claimed monopoly on human organization. It alternates between trying to lick the Church and trying to join it; persecution is followed by establishment. In one mood, the Powers tell us that voluntary assent is a mirage, and our only choice is to come over and humanize their coercion. In another mood they congratulate us on our discovery; and then come over and introduce their coercion into the Church, turning it into one more department of State. The Church characteristically makes the mistake of fighting the last war instead of this one. The push for a secular Christianity today is the last gasp of the Reformation; the big enemy is still seen as a coercive self-centered Church. But that enemy is dead. The real enemy is our temptation to join the State in its enterprise, instead of carrying out our proper and different enterprise.

The task of our time, to which the Church has the only adequate clues, is to create a web of voluntary noncoercive relations as a counter-organization of human society over against the States—and their house-organ the United Nations. Of course a lot of what claims to be the Church is really the State; and a lot of what really is the Church goes under different names or none. The Beast has his claws so deep in us that we have to mobilize all our resources to burn out his mark from our forehead.

Our love can't be satisfied with anything less than a declaration of sacred war against the Establishment—that paradoxical campaign which alone can be called defensive or just. We are to put on the complete guerrilla outfit of truth. Only our newly found unity in the radical Jesus will give us a fighting chance to persevere. Even so, many are likely to fall—especially those struggling in the dark with mixed-up orders. The two things which will most commend recruitment in our army are the services we perform for the victims of war, and the dignity with which we submit to our own casualty status. Performing and accepting ministry are the two sides of the coin which is the genuine human stamp, held together by the solidarity in which we bear one another's burdens.

chapter EIGHT

The Demand to Help: Waiting on Table

We identify with another person by casting him in the closest role inside our family, as substitute father, son, wife, sister, uncle. Our relationship acquires reality either by our joint work on some team, or through some modification of sexuality. It reflects the emotions and tensions of my family; likewise, as in the family, I see through the relation what I was once or will be.

In particular, one man gets under another's skin as substitute *brother;* comrade, master, or apprentice, depending on age. If I find myself diminished or shrivelled by the identification, I'm seeing my brother as *victim* and suffering with him. If I feel a block in the identification, he enters into the peculiar relation of being my *enemy;* instead of the fraternal support of David and Jonathan, I feel the rivalry of Cain and Abel.

The Need for Subordination

My perception of the brother as enemy reveals a fault in myself. If our analysis of history is correct, we should be persuaded that the enemy's side will lose and that our side will win. If he threatens us even so, it's a sign we've left out some important consideration, for which we should be thankful to him. But if we've truly done our homework, we should see in the enemy one more casualty of the System, deprived by it of his manhood. It's just that he doesn't know it and resists awareness.

The enemy is a special kind of victim. The suburb is a ghetto victimized by frustration and fear, and can send out distress-signals only through its children. The powerful are the object of hatred, mostly justified, from all around the world. There isn't any standard by which they can be called successful or fulfilled human beings.

We have the options of rejecting or accepting identification with the helpless victim. So far as we're afraid of sinking to his level, we reject him and become *his* enemy, striking him down with our heel to increase the distance between us. Almost every white person in America is objectively racist; he maintains inviolate some refuge, social or vocational, from which the black is excluded. Seeing the injustice of his own side, he knows that in strict fairness a complete reversal of positions is called for. He's afraid that the first step towards righting the wrong would set that whole wheel turning; and so he's not before taking the step.

This complicity is only overcome through enforcing the identification by an act of will. This obviously means helping the victim—treating him as a blood brother, as we in empathy would like to be treated. The "altruism" of the Golden Rule is the conclusion of a syllogism, whose premises are our own needs and the solidarity of the race. Built into our makeup is the demand to be permitted *service*. Essential to its reality is that we should have something to help the victim with, we don't come empty-handed.

We have our own world: our kids who like to go on walks and bring home frogs' eggs; our students who want to know what we've read; people we like to sing with. If we haven't got anything to bring the victim from that world, where is the reality in our offer to be his servant? Great men have fallen into this trap. Albert Schweitzer still maintained a bush hospital when Africans wanted medical centers; he didn't offer them the things *he* lived for, Bach and Biblical criticism. Through his partial failure we may judge the authenticity of *our* service. If the victim asks for revolution, we'll at least try to redistribute land. And we can be sure that he's also asking to give *us* something—in any case, the meaning of his suffering.

The System feels a threat in our demand to help—a deep relationship which bypasses its mode of operation. So it makes the conditions of service unpleasant and leaches out ideological content. Social workers are underpaid and overloaded; subjected to harrassing regulations, like their clients; forced to spend half their time writing reports under the county official who has graciously allowed them the privilege of service. They're not allowed to share anything valuable with the client—common artistic projects, friendship, study, religious or political activities. No wonder there's a high casualty rate among workers. The sensitive break down after a few years, make a mess of their own lives, become exhausted or cynical. Worse yet for all parties if they adjust to the job by becoming hard-boiled.

Alternatively, the System co-opts service for its own ends. The Peace Corps sends young people with a desire for service off to foreign lands that the State Department is interested in, for a period short enough to keep them from becoming a revolutionary force there. But nobody anticipated the radicalizing effect on the young people, who on their return can't enter conventional vocations, and become a revolutionary force *here*. The Government overreached itself in exposing them to reality. We now hear talk about universal youth training, centered of course on military "service"—as if the art of killing bore some relationship to the figure of the waiter at table.

Chaplaincy as the Corruption of Service

The co-option of service is perfected in *chaplaincy*. The chaplain's clients are inmates of a place of involuntary servitude: a boys' school, a prison, an old folks' home, an army, a mental institution, a juvenile hall. The chaplain is dispensed by the warden from any prior vows which imply an authority superior to the institution. In return for permission to make impersonal contact with his charges under supervision, and to help them circumvent minor regulations, he's assigned his real role as spiritual policeman: maintaining discipline, inculcating the spirit of the institution, building morale. When relatives or reporters ask about conditions in the punishment compound or infirmary, the chaplain is available as front man.

The American middle class *is* middle class because it instinctively pays that deference to the System which penal institutions must enforce. A widespread seminary joke (and dream) is a call for the ministry to the overprivileged. Not surprising then that it shares all features of chaplaincy but coercion. The military-industrial complex maintains the housing development as its place of involuntary servitude. More and more the once invisible stockade separating it from the ghetto is marked with real barbed

wire. Its plan from the beginning provided for denomina-
tional churches of appropriate architecture and well-
indoctrinated chaplains, to soften the private blows of life,
and to keep the inmates of the magnolia compound adjusted, efficient, ignorant, and guilty.

Even as we work to destroy exploitation in the future,
we must patch up its damage in the present. But service
can never be politically neutral. While our political parti-
sanship must always be provisional, it must also be ex-
plicit. Even the alleged services of the chaplain are in the
end phony; neither the military resister nor the boarding-
school rebel consults him. Rather than try to convert him,
we pull strings for radical clergy to visit the disenfranchised in military stockades or youth-prisons, and publi-
cize what they find. Lyndon Johnson and Ronald Reagan
did what decades of preaching had failed at: they *nigger-
ized* white moralists so that they could say truly, "We are
all street people; we are all Viet Cong." Only through naturalization in the ghetto and the colony do we lay claim to
our humanity; we're constituted by the black, the hippy.

The warden finds the chaplain useful and contempti-
ble; the terms of their relationship ensure that the chaplain won't have a message for him. Only the Gospel agitator has a chance of getting through. Another time he's
likely to show up as inmate; the depth of his influence depends on his consistency in the two roles. Only he can get
through the elephant-hide and bring the sword of the
Spirit to the violent oppressor—of all men most oppressed
by his own violence. Only the radical independent is free
enough to treat the men with revolvers not as pigs but as
people.

If the Man is denying basic human needs to the oppressed—food, clothing, shelter, medicine—in Biafra or Berkeley, then the agitator goes out with those necessities. But at a certain point he realizes that he's working for the authorities, who rely on him to cool it for them. As political consciousness increases among the oppressed—partly as a result of his own presence—a point comes where they still ask him for those needs, but despise him if he offers nothing more. Now he must find something else to give them; only his own motivation is good enough in the end.

The Waiter at Table

The central novelty introduced by Jesus was making the type of human merit the waiter at table, the *diakonos*. From the Latin names of the servant and slave come the words by which we generalize this notion, *ministry* and *service*. He so sees himself, "I am among you as one that serves," and is seen by others, "taking the form of a slave." His way means willingness to feed the hungry and give the child a cup of water. He is credited with indefinite powers to feed people and provide drink. Unquestionably he had indefinite powers of curing psychosomatic diseases; the record provides little which resembles invention. Especially plausible is the slight importance he is shown as attaching to these powers.

In his absolute respect for the neighbor, he sees corporal works of mercy as pointing to a new transaction between the hidden power of history and each individual, where he is only the catalyst. For the first time, people were taking on the human shape intended from the beginning. His final service is giving them a name for that new state of affairs. He puts them on exactly the same level as himself, making no secret of his own motivation. Each is to go out in turn and take on the same role of servant. With the same order of priorities: they also are to heal and feed, but above all convey their own understanding of that mission.

The good news of which they're heralds is that human fulfilment in community comes by the act of service. And conversely; the highest service lies in the act of announcing none other than that good news. In one series of teachings the beneficiary is the anonymous and probably thankless victim. In another series he is the enemy— who as we've seen is also victimized by his own violence. In a world of hardened enmities, nothing short of actual reconciliation will do.

No religion less priestly than this. Reversal of hierarchy runs through the whole record. No individual or group is pre-eminent. Texts of shaky authenticity point to one Peter or a Twelve as pronouncers of forgiveness. A text of higher authority makes the duty and power of forgiveness universal: "Forgive us our oppressions *to the extent that* we have forgiven our oppressors." The harlots and quislings go into the area of liberation ahead of religious leaders. When we finally find a passage where leaders are being appointed, what are the conditions of their leadership? They're the ones who are regularly seen washing their brothers' feet, "He who is great among you shall be the least." The one sign of pre-eminence is subordination.

So the Messianic status of Jesus was the fact that a prostitute anointed him for death. Paul agrees that the central item of Jesus' "ministry" was neither his symbolic actions nor his carefully assembled words, but his destined death. Still there must come a class of men (very likely the least important of all) with a traditional literary education, who do the verbal communicating that's also needed, naming what others are doing. To this class alone in the usage of later generations the title of "ministry" has stuck. It's true that their subordination is also the only role which their teacher claims for himself; by their unimportance they have a closeness to him. In the paradoxes of modesty there's no place to speak of greater or lesser, but only of different functions in the one body.

Today we realize uneasily that waiters, like taxicab drivers, are thinking about their tip; their availability is controlled by union regulations. Where shall we find the servant? The friendly bartender doubles as bouncer; the available psychiatrist marks down his thirty-five bucks an hour. The only person who puts himself unreservedly at the service of others is the clown. The brash repartee with which he cons us out of our spare change is only part of the act. Like the waiter he has a complicated routine which it takes a lifetime to master. Shakespeare learned from some sacral tradition that only the Fool could be the chorus of the tragedy; but who told America that every circus must have its clown? He's the last prophet with immunity to prick the follies and crimes of the powerful.

The Problem of Leadership

The need for clear lines of leadership in any organization is obvious. Equally persuasive is the radical way the Gospel overthrows our accustomed notions of leadership.

It's a problem of maximum difficulty to adjust the claims of organization and of the Spirit without falling into either anarchy or papacy. The difficulty isn't arbitrary. Both as a theoretical and a practical problem, it's the hardest first step in embodying the new way into an actual community. Here if anywhere can we be confident that we're dealing with the breakage of orders at the root. We can say in advance that any alleged form of ministry must constantly be justifying its existence. When one fails to, as it will from time to time, the actual place of ministry will move elsewhere. There isn't any external sign other than itself that it can certainly be recognized by.

The most primitive form of community, gathering food or making war or opening up a cave, presupposes leadership, a rudimentary politics. The final form of community rejects the political leadership of coercion; it accepts the fact of leadership, but turns it upside down by making it a primacy in service. No legally defined office can guarantee its holder the reality of being a "servant of the servants of God"; Popes are where we find them. Since we must always hold back from supporting political leaders, all the more we need a kind of leadership which in principle we can accept without qualification. That doesn't prevent us from doubting the reliability of a particular individual or institutionalized ministry; it does mean that the idea of ministry isn't flawed at the root like political leadership.

The Twelve Apostles weren't Elders and they weren't ordained. They just set the example of the servant who washes the guests' feet, the volunteer who takes our place in the gas chamber. They're told that the same role is played wherever somebody casts out demons in the name of Jesus—a man's name being what defines his character. The cloudy Presbyters, Deacons, Bishops of the Apostolic Age were a good translation of the idea of ministry; but they were a translation, the thing which has to be done in every age. Ministry in our age is translated into the figure of Gandhi, the medical heroes of *The Plague,* this one and that one in whom we recognize it. The only valid Apostolic Succession is the history of love. Whatever community we finally anchor in will be found to have authentic roots in that history.

The Gospels radically overthrow all ecclesiastical pretensions; the only authenticity of ministry is faithfulness to the pattern of service in Jesus. The enormous breakthrough of the Ecumenical Movement, which we're just beginning to appreciate, is that *any claim to ministry can be presumed in advance legitimate.* Mutal subordination is the ministry shared by the human race; it's the only way we can put the orders back together again, starting with society. The genuineness of any ordination is the clarity with which it illustrates that universal ordination. Any ministry is as valid as it chooses.

In the first centuries of the Church, the biggest problem was a claim to legitimacy by mythological syncretistic cults promising a private salvation. To meet them, it was important for the ministry to trace its authority back in time through a *continuity of teaching* to the Apostles. From Constantine through the Middle Ages, the authority of the ministry as a matter of practice rested on *political authentication* in the present by a hierarchical society. The Reformers judged a church and its ministry by the fidelity of its preaching the *Epistle to the Romans*; and, in the case of Calvin, by its conformity to a (precariously)

reconstructed New Testament pattern of church-organiza-
tion. Over against this archaeological claim to restore a
forgotten past, the Catholic Church alleged a *continuity of
ordination* back to the Apostles. But all parties were in the
unconscious trap of asking for a sort of validity parallel to
that of the new nations. Only the radical Reformation sects
and their successors tried to break loose into conformity
with the actual circumstances of the New Testament.

The Ecumenical Movement was made possible
through the breakdown of the alliance between Church
and State invented by Constantine. Since the Church is no
longer integrated into the State's legal system, the ministry
no longer has to present its legal qualifications. When political powers are contending for control of the State, it's a
life-and-death matter that individuals should be given
guidance about recognizing the correct one. The valida-
tion of political regimes—of course by a legal system of
their own creation—is their essence. When the State relied
on one or more captive churches to give it legitimacy, the
same notion of validity was automatically applied to them
also.

Now that Christendom is again a community set over
against the State, as when it was born, each of these standards for an authentic ministry can be used where it works.
The Church now being liberated will recognize a *continuity* with everything good in its past—particularly with the
succession of saints. It will let its forms be influenced by
the *political structures* to which it has most commitment
—namely, revolutionary ones. With the Reformers, it will
judge its message by *conformity to the New Testament*.
But not (like the official Reformation) in Paul's interpretation; rather (like the radical Reformation) in the words

of Jesus. It will also look to the New Testament for the *form of ministry;* not as a fixed hierarchy of offices (which can't be found there), but as conformity to the non-self-assertion of Jesus.

Today any group that claims to be a Christian community should be accepted as such until proved otherwise. People aren't lining up to grab the coattails of the Church; what would be gained by a false claim to faith? So likewise the minister accepted by some community has an advance presumption in his favor. But society, in face of the threat which service presents to it, undercuts ministry by treating the servants as if they were masters through social-security exemptions, tax deductions, draft immunity, social perquisites. The claim to those benefits is the only warning signal against a purported ministry.

Looking at the varieties of experimentation beside the dying trunk of the old churches, we can't tell yet which will be the main channels of the new sap. But we know in principle that if we do today's job, scattered efforts will in time cohere, new forms more adequate to renewal will spring up. With our new historical understanding, we see that this was also how the Apostolic ministry won recognition. We can see how past ages of the Church stiffened impromptu administrative measures into absolutes. We understand too well how prophetic authority is institutionalized to be wholly unaware when it happens again in our midst. Thus we move a step in self-knowledge beyond the Reformation. Institutional forms are more nearly under our control because we understand better their independent life. We'll be more cautious this time about attributing final validity to the forms which turn out correct for our age.

The peculiar mixture of jobs, thought of as equally permanent, held by the American clergyman is an accident of history which needn't last very much longer. Is there a good reason why a man should take on marriage-counselling as a lifetime vocation, or organizing the oppressed, or pulling drunks off streets, or maintaining architectural monuments? The exhausting genuine jobs would perhaps be better done with regular replacements.

Even among the jobs which imply lifetime training or commitment, we should allow wide variations how far they need be united in one person. In fact they're mostly separated today. For example. *Learning in the Bible* or church history: knowledge and love of the old languages, with the generalizing eye to see them mirrored in current experience. *The prophetic voice:* speaking the words which will isolate demonic forces and coordinate resistance to them. *Pastor to the pastors:* recognizing one's own dispensability, enabling colleagues to win actual independence, holding oneself available to help with the personal problems they can't solve for themselves. *Celebration:* the work of the poet and artist who find the right forms for contemporaries to praise existence.

On these criteria, George Fox and John Bunyan (for example), with their irregular authorization, have the best possible claims to a valid ministry. As our problems are more far-reaching, we should expect the true ministry to our age to emerge from our experience with equal surprise and inevitability. If we ask what individual or body ordained the minister, we should be prepared to hear as from Paul that his ordination wasn't of man but of God.

The Ministry of Women

Charles Williams, operating with a sacrificial theory of the common meal, said that women were debarred from offering the blood of Christ symbolically because in the coinherence of the human race they offered it actually. Since the childbirth and care which only they can perform is a uniquely concrete form of service, it's less important to devise other forms for them than for men. Because the center of the Church's celebration is a dramatic representation of what a man once did, propriety of casting will normally have it performed by a male. But female roles could be much more prominent in liturgical or guerrilla theatre on the model of the Christmas mysteries. If the pressure of exclusion is taken off, we should expect women to determine their own level in the universal ordination to service, with some functional specialization over against men, but also with considerable overlap. The mistake has been the assumption of Constantinian Christianity that there must be some one legally defined hierarchy of ministers, rather than the thing which Paul describes so clearly, a coordinated spectrum of talents.

Problems of the Missionary

From the viewpoint of the Third World, what services can be better provided by Westerners than by their own people? In the undeveloped Arab countries, there is room for tactful suggestions about agriculture, sanitation, medicine; for agitation against slavery, virtual or actual. In North Viet Nam, these things have been taken in hand along local lines; heavy industry is being supplied by Socialist countries. But after the war, American radicals could help open up areas of political freedom within the new national unity. Others will judge better what can be done in other lands.

The most essential task has been barely defined: the cultural ambassador. Not as today setting up enclaves to disseminate an alien culture, a Goethe Institut or U.S. Information Service. I look to see urban planners analyzing village societies to see where we went wrong. Or biologists, to study how traditional practice recycles raw materials. Or Western monks going out for dialogue on the inner life. If the appearance of indigenous Eastern churches were in the cards as a result of such meetings, they would appear; no other kind of Oriental church is worth thinking about.

Opening our convictions to other people raises the question: How do we avoid indoctrination, imposing our private or Western styles on others? First by making sure that our views are rooted in an objective analysis of real current needs, actual facts of nature and history. Then, by making sure that what we're recommending, even if possibly erroneous, is at least harmless. In the end we'll find ourselves saying, *Harmlessness is truth.* Not the passive harmlessness of the helpless victim or gagged liberal, but the active reconciling harmlessness for which another name is revolutionary nonviolence. This is just one more way of rephrasing the good news we've been entrusted with—which in the end must carry its authentication on its face.

The World Community of Reconciliation

Saul Alinsky, community organizer, observed that concrete service to obvious human need is the thing which legitimates any more radical action. We go around after the System picking up its pieces, taking the logic of its mistakes more seriously than it does. This is a constructive way of expressing our solidarity with it in error. At the same time it prevents the System from wholly disowning us. Although it will fire us, beat us up, get us in trouble, it can't deny that we're the ones who are washing its dirty dishes. Also the salvaged community constitutes our organizing base, to which we offer a higher level of service: our own understanding of things, our own motivation.

One big threat to America's self-image is the growing army of dropout clergy and sisters. It was they originally who instructed the young people about love and war. Neither teacher nor student could continue school as usual when they discovered that the churches had no intention of taking seriously what was written in their own charter. Society can get indignant at the young people, who were never intended to listen in church, but only go through the motions. But it specifically assigned the clergy the duty of sincerity—and at the same time the incompatible one of getting along with existing conditions. Their withdrawal has had less influence because they've fallen into the posture expected of them, as the victim keeps step with the executioner. The dropout tacitly accepts his assigned role of adulterer, neurotic, doubter; it's harder than we think to escape type-casting. But one day the untidy ranks of the displaced will brace up spontaneously into a community whose outlaw status is a source of pride rather than guilt.

The American church complex assigns its members the duty of bringing reconciliation to all the people they come in touch with. That covers a lot of ground; who on the planet has failed to be contacted by an American Christian? In our one world, the Church has finally rediscovered her original constituency, populations thought permanently silent—grapepickers, ragpickers, ghetto unemployed, prisoners, dispossessed peasants, students, lepers, those social lepers the hippies. Actual reconciliation would be to determine the issue of justice truthfully between the newly vocal and their better-established opponents (many of whom sit in the front pew on Sunday morning), while finding a definition of their common interest they could agree on.

Of course the mediator standing between the lines of street people and a police riot is likely to get hit by rocks, bottles, clubs, bayonets, bullets, chemical agents. He takes that risk. Intelligent Americans should decide though: do they want him there or not? They must realize (like intelligent Russians) that hearts and minds must actually be won, and that it won't work to dispatch tanks into cities, order airstrikes, burn down the houses of peasants, or even send bank credits to the poor. Only men and women will do. The mediator must first win the rebel's trust, and the holders of big power can't offer much advice. They can just choose between two alternatives: putting actual confidence in the messenger of reconciliation who makes his risky trip across lines, or rejecting his offices and waiting for the man with the bandolier carrying an ultimatum.

Those new communities of the alienated in their

dawning self-consciousness speak louder than books the word which the church Establishment has to hear. The irregular ministry to the oppressed by persons with unstable private lives is, more than any other one thing, building the united ministry in the future renewed Church. And our ultimate service of renewal—restoration of the planetary environment—can only be the work of a world reconciling community.

Everyone so far as he can manage his own problems has the potential of becoming a leader. But sooner or later everyone succumbs to his own problems; "Others he saved, himself he cannot save." The other side of the coin of helpfulness is the mental attitude with which we accept the unpleasant reality, either that nobody is helping us, or that we'll have to accept help from somebody. In the end the parabola of our life brings us back again to the mute resentful dependence in which we were born.

chapter NINE

The Demand for Hope: Falling Casualty

As if to make sure we won't be stood up on our date with death, we keep holding rehearsals—falling casualty. Our failures cover a wide band of things we're responsible for and things we aren't; from the inside they look a lot alike. It's hard for a woman to discover by herself whether she's being shelved by her husband, or whether she nags at him and arranges for him to fail, or whether they've both just been given a bum break by the universe.

The child, secure with organs he's too weak to overload, parts whose full function he can only guess, doesn't doubt his immortality. That innocence points to the continuity of the species, of culture—perhaps to some deeper continuity of every instant. But first he must discover that some day his friend the garbage-collector won't come, that he won't always live in this house, that mummy and daddy won't always be there to keep it from burning down while he's asleep; that some day he'll have to turn in the library card which was stamped Permanently Valid. (The reason adults stay up late at night is because *their* mummys and daddys aren't there to keep the house from burning down, they don't trust it to take care of itself.) As dizziness on ladders sets in, we start doing something constructive about it: putting together photograph albums, collecting current American coins, contributing brass flower-stands to the church. Even so not quite constructive enough.

Still we do all need to move over and make room for a new crop to grow up. Some kind of acquiescence or death-wish is built into us. Some people move smoothly towards their destination, dropping off excess baggage at each airport as they use up the final panels of their yard-long excursion ticket. But it's harder to preserve that steadiness in the face of dissolution when we're committed to social change. Both justified guilt and unjustified anxiety become more intense. We can't see what kind of a world we're launching our kids into—with even more inadequate preparations than usual. Will the rainstorm wait until we've closed down the house?

The Rising Casualty-Rate

The types of casualty characteristic in any society point to its areas of greatest tension. The Gospels presuppose a world whose problem is impotence: they're full of lame, blind, paralytics, deaf, dumb, unclean. Paul sees correctly that these are all nonverbal signals of inability to find the right way and hold to it. One class of *our* diseases is a compulsive overloading of the system: heart attacks, cirrhosis of the liver, emphysema. Another is invasions of the organism by a foreign element: allergy, homosexuality, cancer. Both types loom large in our symbolism, we spend the most money dealing with them; perhaps we're even most susceptible to them. What we fear most for our society, with good reason, is collapse from overloading inside, and invasion by foreign elements, outside agitators.

Our nervous breakdowns and family breakdowns are the little snaps which add up to social breakdown. The sado-masochism of bullying and Yesmanship in business illustrates our foreign policy. Our most widely used remedy, the tranquilizer, points to the peace the world is calling for. But we try for it by covering up our awareness of conflict and injustice, rather than by pushing through to the end. We cry Peace Peace where there isn't any peace.

In the movement for social change, casualties of every sort are constant. A man who seemed committed to the way of persuasion begins under stress to speak darkly of guns. A couple who've made big sacrifices for each other, when they're finally reunited and set up in an apartment, after a few months can't keep going and split. A social worker grossly neglects his own family, turns to drugs. The clergyman whose radical project is sabotaged by his superiors, or by its intrinsic difficulty, takes pains to hasten its failure, and in cynicism goes back to selling insurance.

The progressive decay of personal relations, bad enough in a loveless marriage, gets worse under the umbrella of ideology, when both parties can include among their charges against the other side its taking an incorrect line. And then the progressive creation of misunderstandings; treating the other party like a public meeting; each pushing the other into defending an unattractive corner. All our psychic stability, and the vocational second strings to our bow, are needed to stay out of the box, to extricate ourselves once in, to help the others now shut up in it.

But the sign that some kind of revolution will go

through is that ex-radicals aren't swinging onto the conservative bandwagon. They crawl into an apolitical hole and lick their wounds. Our perception of the System's violence can't be shrugged off once we've felt it, even though we succumb or take on counter-violence. Our casualties aren't the gross moral failure of apostasy, finking out, but a gross emotional inadequacy, with unfairness to family and friends. Nobody is better aware of the unfairness than the casualty—which only intensifies his guilt.

Across America (not to go farther afield) is a fellowship of millions who have fallen. If they could be made aware of their brotherhood and set back on their feet again, they'd be an irresistible army. Their recuperation is slow, partial, with many scars; they work themselves back into mechanical undemanding jobs, superficial personal relationships. Still in their silence they raise an incoherent demand that their failure should be made a solid foundation of hope.

Changing What Can Be Changed

A well-known prayer asks for the serenity to accept what can't be changed, the courage to change what can be, and the wisdom to know the difference. This sentiment has been taken up by Alcoholics Anonymous, and we might think about alcoholism for a moment as a typical Establishment form of casualty. One implied dogma is that alcoholism can be changed; we may heartily agree, recognize AA as a disguise of the Church, and help our straight friends make their way to it. Behind this however lies another dogma, that the *tendency* towards alcoholism is something which can't be changed. AA comes close to chaplaincy, assuming that the conditions of society are beyond change, beyond criticism, and that the only possible service is to pick up the pieces. But alcoholism is a groping towards the inner revolution, an honorable though destructive response to the psychic violence of the System. When a person is trapped in a spiral of activities that are destroying his integrity, and still has unfinished business which prevents him killing himself, he resorts to the deferred suicide of drinking. AA, though among the best of Establishment services, still, by sending its members back rehabilitated to the world of fraternal orders and Little League baseball, is only patching up the symptoms of the exploitative system which produced alcoholism in the first place.

But we're never allowed to set limits of possible change in the renewal of institutions or environment. No use bandaging the ulcer unless we treat the infection with antibiotics. Whatever is necessary must be possible. That doesn't prove the change can be effected through us; it does prove we have to try harder and then let somebody else try.

The two sides have only just engaged each other here; the paranoia of the System also strongly infects all who've gotten off the trolley-car tracks of society. The founders of student movements, intentional communities, service-ministries, expect their corps of volunteers to work as a team, and are naively surprised when deep anger or self-deception surfaces over office space and subsistence-allowances. A group apparently must have its quota of such failures before it can see its way to absolutely clear and realistic goals, resolute commitment, an actually functioning organization. Up on the timberline of the future we're too exposed to the elements to allow that hatred of self and of others which the System has bred in.

After that famous fresh start we'd assumed we were now immunized against evil; we could push through on our own projects, accept all the junk the world would dump on us, and have strength left over to help our brothers in trouble. Just then word comes in roundabout that we've hurt somebody's feelings, and he resents it too much to talk about it. Here is where we must remember that the fresh start was meant to be constantly repeated; we must summon up our will and go back to the point we thought we'd left far behind. Although it's not precisely in *our* power to do this, the power is available to make bad personal relations one of the things that can and must be changed.

Accepting the Necessity of Our Failure

But not forever. The capacity of each to absorb punishment and start over again is finite. Happy is the man whose physical strength rides on into a wise old age, and whose moral strength grows to the end. But most of us, not altogether by our own fault, at some point will be hurt so seriously that we won't recover complete use of the injured faculty, even though we may go on some ways further. At some point we'll be hurt so seriously that we *won't* go on much further. This is one of the things we won't change.

With the same broad perspective we bring to the embittered casualty, we can try not to become embittered ourselves. Our insight wasn't all that exceptional. If we, with our mediocre talents, discovered some urgent job and made a try at it, perhaps, if we avoided gross compromises, others will take the same route. Maybe they're just waiting politely for us to get out of the way. The biggest service we can do them is not to add cynicism of ours to their burden, and to express confidence that the job will be done.

Here lies the center of what may be called our spirituality. When we've fallen casualty, by a dull but always possible act of will we may summon up the presence of others who held out to the end. Perhaps those who immolated themselves for justice or peace: Venerable Quang Duc the Buddhist of Saigon, Jan Palach under the Soviet occupation of Prague, our own Norman Morrison the Quaker. Probably we should affirm that this is never the optimum response. All the more then we have to match their firmness as they moved towards the irrevocable act.

As we sink deeper into casualty we may remember that we once planned to be famous. Morrison and the others are remembered by accidents of publicity. At the same time then we should also maintain psychic identification with the anonymous victims of violence—the Holy Innocents of Jerusalem, of the Wars of Religion, the Albigenses, Indians and Negroes, victims of Auschwitz, Coventry, Dresden, Tokyo, Hiroshima and Nagasaki, Viet Nam—as well as those who weren't even caught up in that much history.

Around retirement time we have to face also the status, not of being forgotten in the future, but of being disenfranchised in the present. As usual the problem is interlocking: the false independence of the old, which is really a withdrawing into isolation; the unreal wish of children to perfect their harmonious career before settling a parent down into it. Making the right gesture of good-will to the old is part of the realism with which we later will accept casualty status ourselves.

Whatever happens, we can remember with thankful-ness that we weren't those casualties from birth, the blind and deaf sons of privilege who bring their own special attaché-case sophistication into making counterinsurgency humane. I cut myself once shaving when I remembered suddenly that I'd known quite well the man who gave the order for the bombing. The most intractable and central problem, how such a person can be helped to turn towards the light, is the one about which there seems the least to say. We haven't any reason to feel we're better than he is; we can just be grateful for the luck, or providence, which made us more vulnerable to the truth.

Although our casualty may be a physical separation from the community which is working for change, we can know that we're never cut off from somebody who's been genuinely our brother. The successful have made their graves already in their life; but the memory of the martyr, the clown, the fanatic, the fool is always green. We go to join the honorable company of all who chose the risk that their weakness would be revealed—and were gravely taken up on that bet by the Universe.

Sacred Casualty

Suddenly at the end of the day we remember with hope that our elder brother was also a failure. All along, the mark of his casualty status has been hanging around our necks; it's identical with our struggle for peace. Briefly during his life he seemed to have persuaded the others about the new way; then political interests regained the upper hand in their minds and he lost them. Any formulations he may have developed about how he'd do his job must have fallen away from him, and there's little evidence he found any clear substitute. So we lose the original fresh certainty of our convictions, and are left holding the empty carton of an enterprise without contents. The one thing we can hold on to is that we're the latest in a long line of failures; better so than in what is called the world's long line of successes.

At this point, our casualty, without ceasing to be itself, starts getting turned upside down in the massive reversal which history makes of all the world's values. As usual our end recapitulates our beginning. Here where the trajectory of our rocket reapproaches the earth it set out from, once again a fresh start is indicated. In our weakness we're to reaffirm the correctness of the vision we were guided by in our original strength. The united power of our weakness down through history overthrows every working principle of the men in button-down shirts who are thought to determine the course of affairs. In the paradoxical interchange of rich and poor, master and servant, high and low, first and last, the clown also shakes up our conventional notions about life and death in his hat, and turns them onto the table in a quite unsuspected relationship.

The record shows failure and execution followed by a kind of success where legend finds itself at a loss for words, which for want of a better name we call resurrection. New life appears as solidarity of a brotherhood. When the fraternal relations catalyzed by some third party survive the worst the world can do to them, there's no way to avoid their continuing operation in the affairs of men. The earthbound individual body is metamorphosed into a weightless winged phase everywhere visible. In another part of the record, that change is anticipated in the living body as transfiguration (just a Latin translation of "metamorphosis"). The pattern of our hope is given on the fragrant mountain which to our middle age had loomed as hopeless fatigue, swinging open like a gate of dream to the secret valley. We feel the foldings of the earth's crust dynamically as an actual pushoff to the stars. The Hudson Valley is realized in nineteenth-century woodcuts as Bunyan's Delectable Mountains. Still the mountain-gates don't cease being the gates of death as well, and we'll not forget that Transfiguration is also Hiroshima day.

After many false starts, one day we discover that the ferry-boat has finally left the mainland and is headed for an indistinct shoreline out to sea. The last cars are on board, the gulls soar silently looking at our sandwiches. The propellers are veining the water into alabaster, surprising schools of tiny fish. The seabreeze smelling of fish and tar pushes back the land heat. We sit among children, bird-watchers, businessmen in sports shirts going through newspapers, detached and forgetting whether the ferry is taking us to the Fortunate Isles of a Martha's Vineyard or to another commuter job. Our credit cards are in our pocket and we've left a note for the people who are taking our house; but there's been no word from the uncommunicative Yankee agent who manages our summer affairs. And it turns out our services were not all that indispensable at the office. Finally the conduct of affairs is out of our hands.

Building the Casualty-List into a Community

The ultimate discreditation of the churches as they exist is their callousness and inability to deal with casualties inside or outside. The only salvage operation we may be able to mount is joining the refugees in the rubble. Even that is some gift. Those we rehabilitate may not seem the best material to built a resilient organization from; still there they are, an available manpower pool.

Our big mistake is confusing casualty-status with refutation of our principles or methods. Properly we should see it as irrefutable proof of both; we had hold of such a big chunk of reality that the System couldn't tolerate us any longer. When somebody freaks out we shouldn't panic and call in the head-shrinker or get a lot of pills prescribed. Rather, take it as one more incentive to develop a psychiatry or cure of souls which will help people live with not being adjusted to their society, and turn their energies to changing it.

In the end, whether this or that renewal succeeds depends how far all kinds of people—conservative, confused, bluecollar—can see it as fulfilling their own suppressed hopes. The deepest effect of any movement is on those who touch it only at its outermost fringes where its apparent force is fully spent. At that point, with absolute accuracy a collective unconscious symbolism picks out the true center of a man's work—George Fox's hat, Francis' birds, Gandhi's spinning-wheel.

The community we dream of is neither a sect turned in on itself nor the old System lightly sprinkled with reform. It has to be none other than the actual society of man, with all its confused history and destructive tendencies, waking up and turning to the sunlight that streams in the windows. If the dispossessed convince us too completely we'll pull out; if we convince the authorities too completely we'll sell out. Renewal wavers between the poles of a fatal magnetism: separatism and co-option. Failure is the only way to avoid both and insure that our work is appropriated simply by the one community of men and women.

In the end, success or failure isn't ours to decide on. We have bread if the earth grows it. But we can always by an act of will focus our eye on the needs of the present, with the wisdom provided by a firm hold on the living vine of the past. The central content of that remembrance is that *defeat means solidarity*. Through our embrace of casualty we choose life.

chapter TEN

The Demand
for Joy:
The Feast

It's something less than a pun to say that since our lives are maintained by assimilation, fulfilment must mean being filled full. In the warm Mediterranean climate, which lies behind us, there isn't the need for constant intake of calories to keep up body temperatures. Breakfast or lunch just keep the stomach going until dinnertime at sunset. When artificial light barely existed, sleep and sexuality came right after the meal—there wasn't anything else to do. (Up until recent times, people slept longer in winter than in summer—the species was semihibernating. The afternoon siesta in part avoids the summer heat, in part makes up for the short sleeping night.) It was at dinner that the basic family community was realized. When people are in good health, not in mourning or facing a coming event with anxiety, even under a repressive political regime it's hard to prevent dinner being a time of actual happiness.

The Realization of Community

One feature of joy is the spirit of play—the extension of childhood into adult life through mock food gathering or mock combat (where conversely for the child, play anticipates adult work). Play is one of the things we do most nearly for its own sake, as Perpetua in her vision of Paradise found nothing else to do. The feast is permanently endowed with something like play through the gift of Dionysos, the sap of the vine "which makes glad the heart of Gods and men." Of all mind-altering chemicals, alcohol alone appeared universally through agriculture and took a place at the common meal. We have only legends about a humanity without wine—which may in fact have helped break the fixed circuits of instinct and start the species on the new path of consciousness. As the horse and dog are built permanently into our psyche through accidents of domestication; the lion and eagle, salmon and stag through symbolism and sport; even more closely the vine trails over all the works of Western man. The lands where it grows with difficulty or hasn't caught on, like China and India, are the most foreign to us; but even they must come to terms with it in the end because of the world-role of Western humanity.

In the ancient city-state the meat-eating Homeric hero or Bedouin is continued as theoretical ideal through occasional animal sacrifice; but the growth of population and poverty forced vegetarianism, supplemented by cheese and fish. The meat-offering of Abel the virtuous nomad is called acceptable over against the grain-offering of agricultural Cain; but this polemic against Canaanite influence was soon overthrown by history. Semitic *laḥm-* "staff of life" denotes meat in Arabic but bread in Hebrew. Roman soldiers marched on two pounds of soggy black bread per diem, and complained if it was replaced by less staying venison. Dependence on grain for life and the vine for meaning led to a sacral apology for cutting them, like the stronger taboos associated with animal blood. (Even more serious to cut a tree, and forests or groves belonged to the god or his political agent.) The yearly death and rebirth of the grain was seen as a hopeful prospect for the men who fed on it. Pindar must refer to the ritual exhibition of an ear of grain at Eleusis:

> Blessed is he who goes under ground having seen these
>   things;
> He knows the end of life,
> And he knows its God-given beginning.

Demeter and Persephone, to have the seed of grain taken around the world, sent out the naked youth Triptolemos, who has reached us as Johnny Appleseed.

The necessities of agriculture led to discovery of the magical number 365, and pegged recurrent celebrations on the year it defined. The strictly lunar calendar of Islam that wanders through the year suits the needs of the night-riding nomad. We were forced into nonlunar "months" by the overriding importance of the year. Still a woman I know remembers the lunar phase when each baby came; and the central festival of our year remains tied to our now violated sister. The ebb and flow of psychic energy also dictated a shorter cycle, once fixed as the four quarters of the moon, which now like the month marches out of phase with the moon, at its mechanical pace of seven days.

As village communities expanded into imperial cities, dates of accession and founding were located on the farm-calendar; the natural biological cycles became the basis of history. So the child learns to define its involvement in the family and nature through festivals at snowtime, flower-time, end of school, and dead-leaf time. It locates its individuality by the recurrent celebration of its own birthday.

The original forms of politics and art cluster around the ceremonies which define the community's meaning. The gathering of the citizen body—whether for war, voting, athletics, or festival—was an assembly of substantially the same group of men (excluding women, children, slaves, and foreigners) in various public places wearing various uniforms. In particular the linen of the festival is taken up, as we saw, in the fresh start of the Church—whose Greek name, *ekklesia,* earlier meant the Assembly of the democratic city. For it saw itself as the commonwealth of those whose city was the universe.

The basic symbolic form of the community was the traditional literary text used as libretto for a ritual drama produced at the festival. It explains by history or myth how the community was founded; it also derives moral principles for contemporary action from that original event. In a regular cycle of secularization the sacred drama is elaborated, separates from the festival, achieves meaning in its own right, and sinks back to formalism or triviality. So Attic drama arose from the cult of Dionysos; European music from the marriage of church music and folk music (itself enshrining a pagan religion); Shakespeare from the English mystery-plays. Today the sacred arts are in the decay phase of the cycle. The limitations of Marxism-Leninism come out strongly in the banality of Soviet public ceremonies. Only the very young find a source of renewal in music produced while under the influence of electricity. Perhaps the unamplified guitars and masked mimes of the peace movement contain the sacred drama of the future.

Meeting the Crisis of Joylessness

How can we bring the alternation of the seasons to life again—snow on the mountains or poppies in the field? Is it possible to think our way back into the Panathenaic procession, high Mass at Chartres, a Fourth of July circus? On this big spaceship that the little ones lift off from, we become aware of orbiting the sun, we acquire a case of motion sickness. To get sea-legs once again we must brace ourselves against the steering-wheel of history. The innovative Zen hippy be-in leaves out the most important thing: continuity with past celebration.

The replacement of natural cycles by arbitrary technique on an automatized globe presents us only with the joyless alternatives of isolation and crowds, anxiety and consumption, affluence and poverty. Information retrieval isn't part of the solution but of the problem; for the knowledge we need to retrieve isn't the kind that can be put on tape, it must exist in the minds and bodies of men. A Greek tragedy *is* classes studying it, scholars writing commentaries on it, academic places painfully staging it in Greek, playwrights adapting it for Broadway. The past slips away from us like the tail of a comet. To hold it in line we must build it into stone, set it to music, rehearse it in our bodies; and then go out in the streets of the future and *do* it in face of the Man's batons and choppers.

If we said correctly that our task is pushing forward a triple revolution, then our celebration must be a call to revolution—or better, a revolutionary act. But in our America *happiness would be a revolutionary act!* That appropriate joy for our age must also say clearly that it isn't the invention of our age or of America, but that it lies at the roots of humanity and isn't lacking from any age, though sometimes covered over pretty deep with our garbage. Affluence makes its celebration a grim display of the status quo. In middle-class liberalism, unproductive experiments in group relations mark the scene. The anti-Establishment world makes its celebration too anti-intellectual, so that it can't *learn* from its joy, and its politics becomes a paranoid factionalism instead of a joyful sharing in action. Celebration vacillates between individual escape and communal euphoria, heightened or blurred in a chemical haze.

Looking at the self-destructive drug scene today—in some form spread across all classes—and thinking back to grossly alcoholic nineteenth-century America, it's easy to sympathize with Methodist total abstinence. But we mustn't forget how the preacher's son was driven in turn back to drunkenness. Every overindulgence signals some defect; medieval gluttony was perhaps trying to compensate for a vitamin-deficient diet. The alcoholism of parents is discredited among alienated youth, who had to find an agent of ecstasy unavailable to their elders—by being illegal. Equally attractive by its vague impropriety is the alleged Oriental mysticism which the young have taken up, spiritual grass, the opiate of the dropout classes.

The ecstasy associated with drugs is in principle legitimate and necessary, since the human race was weaned on wine. But our potent synthetic chemicals reinforce the compulsion of self-manipulation, and many naturally occurring drugs are addictive. To an outsider, the most attractive natural drug would be peyote, both for its spectacular effects and for its rooting in an authentic cult of the oppressed red man. Marijuana is the mildest—because our Cannabis produces it only in strong dilution. Its chief proved danger is its illegality, and certainly existing or proposed penalties for its use are grossly out of line. But its symbolic function for a generation on strike is too much of a hot-house plant, not rooted in history. Since it's not part of a meal it privatizes ecstasy. And its past associations are violent; for in its stronger form of hashish it gave their name to "assassins." It can't compete with Dionysos, whom we're stuck with for better or worse.

There the community feast is at the heart of our tradition. No way to scrap that past and make a new beginning. In no imaginable future can we let the community celebration mesh into political structures, too much injustice is built into them. The community must cut across all social strata and existing politics, as it began long ago. Its unity can't be imposed by an authorized hierarchy or charismatic leader. And all its forms, wherever they come from, will only be adopted on their actual merits, by spontaneous assent, to which legislation and leadership must be subordinated.

The final non-negotiable demand of life is joy; it must reflect both current needs and a central tradition.

That tradition will surely be relevant to our needs, since it was formed precisely in answer to the shadowside of history: a continuity of violence exercised by different agencies, but all under a permanent demonic influence which we can only grasp through the mythology of a global counterinsurgency force. It has twined its masses of parasitic dodder around the green stem of life; celebration must break away from that kiss of death along our entire course.

Celebration as Summing Up Our Trajectory

Each phase of our journey is represented in the festival of celebration, which must do justice to the requirements of all. At the same time each receives from it an extra tonality of happiness.

The fresh start of fidelity. The existing Church fails even to read aloud the standard it proposes to disobey. Cranmer put the definition of conformity to social *mores,* the Ten Commandments, at the beginning of his sacred meal. But already in Jesus' time, enlightened rabbis held that the Law could be reduced to a single principle—not doing to others what you didn't want them to do to you. "What is the most important commandment?" was a conventional question. One tradition says that Jesus volunteered an answer acceptable to the intellectuals: two commandments, love of God and love of neighbor. But Luke is probably right (10: 27) in stating that this was rather the ready-made answer the questioner came with. In either case, Jesus' own original formulation is quite different; it doesn't exactly deny the law of Moses, but it does go beyond it. He introduces the radical novelty of identifying the neighbor as the *victim*. Either the helpless and probably unthankful outcast, as Luke here goes on to indicate; or (even more radically) the *enemy* seen as victim of his own prejudices, shut up in the ghetto of affluence, from whom we expect only hard words and persecution.

If we're to call our community a following of Jesus and not some kind of liberal Judaism, we can only post up as the condition of its fresh start his own teaching, *Love your enemies*. We will make our rule *radical reconciliation*. Even if we wish to interpret those words out of existence, we should be reminded about the starting-point of our exegesis as often as possible. Episcopalians may be interested to find out the one place in their Prayer Book where this imperative is found. In a world which can be destroyed both by the weapons of our enemy and of that neighbor who claims to represent us, loving your enemy is the only prudence. The community festival is a mainspring of action to carry out the spirit of its fresh start.

The community of love. The community is the next bigger level of organization, in which family units are the proper cells. It calls its members brothers and sisters. It contains parallels to all the family relations—sexuality, comradeship, the refined relation between brother and sister. A young man isn't in all that unique a relation to his girl friend, since he tries fitting every other girl into the same role; but his relation to his sister has a unique color. The community gives *all* relations that color. Its tone is hit off, we're told, by the wedding feast; the company celebrates a sexuality not its own, but which as by-product has brought it together.

Since the community will often be a hit-and-run affair, one step ahead of the Man, moving in where change is happening, losing people to jail or travel, its membership will be fluid. It will try to recognize its real members where it finds them, under whatever name. Among people who agree with it about the nonviolent revolution, its task is removing the obstacles to seeing Jesus as founder of the revolution. It will unmistakably call itself a continuation of Jesus—and at the same time welcome anybody willing to accept it in its own spirit.

Above all it'll take pains not to put barriers of *its* making between itself and existing denominations. It will also take pains not to be added to their number, but to be a force working for love in each of them. It will be clear where it stands—in such a way as to make it easiest for them to move in that direction. It will be a community of *radical ecumenism;* not reunion for the sake of administrative tidiness, but for joint action in the necessary jobs of renewal.

No previous age of church history has been in the position of putting together a unity out of petrified fragments. The style of operation needed is so new and flexible, that we can only describe it concretely after it's happened. It's only possible in such a vanguard scene as the United States, with representatives of all traditions shaken loose from traditional assumptions. Its new structures will reject from the old only what it must, and incorporate from the old whatever it can.

The intersection of the vocations. In celebration, history and the arts meet the individual most intimately. The liturgy is its own dance. Liturgies of the West represent the dignity of the Roman patrician in his own house; their items of dress and gesture are our living link to the classical world. The Church also formalizes ecstatic dances of liberation, shaking and quaking; and items of dress like the friar's habit which once identified the wearer as one of the poor. A minister to the twentieth century is a man wearing bluejeans.

Historically we understand how cult builds architecture to house itself. The cathedral of Sicilian Syracuse was built in the fifth century B.C. as a Doric temple to Athena of victory, converted into a basilica under Constantine, briefly given Moorish ornaments, and provided with a baroque façade in the eighteenth century. The American churches where one can see native meaning are the white steeples of New England and the missions of California; but both streams have now run dry.

Classic periods of the Church have a uniquely appropriate music, simple enough for any congregation, deep enough not to be exhausted by any genius. Such were Gregorian plainsong; Lutheran chorale; the English tradition where Watts and the Wesleys are dominant. Nothing is more convincing than a uniform celebration in one of those styles with a choir or congregation to which it's native. Nothing more unconvincing than tasteful eclecticism from all styles in a congregation that can't sing or feel any of them. There's no people's base for church music today except freedom songs and peace songs with guitar accompaniment. But it will be a while before we get a translation of all the things we need to say in that idiom.

If the future holds art-forms representing a new humanity, it will be because, in our age of artistic deprivation, we worked that humanity out without symbolism, in men and women. Through the celebrations of the naked Church which lies ahead we may recover the power of the word. Perhaps the community will pick up its new language already being spoken, from a Bob Dylan, as the folksong of a Trinh Cong Son already speaks the message of peace to all Vietnamese. Anyway it's set the task of *radical translation,* unlocking a treasure-trove of words to say the old things the only way we can hear them. It must find the childhood rhythms, political slogans, formulas of anger or love which will once again sound like men and women talking about their actual concerns.

Since the Church preserves every element of culture in its most original form, its word is a *language of the mouth and ear,* not of the hand and eye. Skimming is the technique of an amphetamine generation which speeds to assimilate more than it really can, on the assumption that meaning is spread thin. We will set up detoxification clinics from those spiritual uppers, and write over the door: SPEED READING KILLS. The ancient book, like modern poetry, is so densely composed it can't be grasped at a rate faster than reading aloud. Our Gospels are compilations of short oral items which at one time circulated independently. Their liturgical reading in those sections continues the way they were first delivered to illiterate audiences, before even they were collected in books.

In the end the word comes to us as a synthesis of the arts. In tonal languages like Vietnamese every sentence has its intrinsic melody; the group recitation of the Lord's Prayer brings its own plainsong. So Pindar composed a simple melody for each ode, and designed a choreography for the boys who sang it, appropriately costumed, in a Doric setting. But before that happens again the word will have to be stripped of everything else and come to us nakedly spoken, nakedly heard. No programmed learning or closed-circuit television will take the place of our brother speaking—speaking precisely because we're there in front of him.

The community as place of sacrifice. The only way of dealing with power is letting it destroy itself through our submission. That way is seemingly broken by the first law of life, assimilation; we are what we eat. The vegetarianism of a Gandhi awakens deep echoes in us before we dismiss it as impractical. Even ancient agricultural societies ate meat on ceremonial occasions. Except in hunting economies the date of the ceremony was fixed on the calendar, and so could only be met by a domesticated animal—itself born at a fixed lambing season. A "domesticated" animal was one living in the house, like the man's ewe lamb in the parable of Nathan. In Moslem Beirut, lambs are still brought in as pets and slaughtered on the festival. The children (and adults too) grow fond of the new family member. Some societies grant it honorary family membership; in others the family is enrolled in a sheep or kangaroo totem. At slaughter-time permission or forgiveness must be asked, on the chance that the animal knows more than we realize. Its killing is the sacred and polluting operation of *sacrifice.*

In the ancient world, temples were the only slaughterhouses. Paul had all that trouble with "meat offered to idols" because there wasn't any other kind. Open sacrifice imposed standards of cleanness publicly verifiable; it also reminded men, if the race must be continued by bloodshed, what bloodshed was like. Our locked slaughterhouses—at best antiseptic, at worst jungles—would have offended classical sensitivities. We lock them up for the same reason we send old folks away to die; we have too bad a conscience about death. But in the Providence of God the TV news has uncovered what we wrapped up.

Puritan America is as addicted to mass slaughter as Assyria or the Third Reich. We tempt Fate by stockpiling fissionable materials, nerve gas all over the planet. The Spanish, in spite of their reputation for ferocity, were the only conquerors of the New World to intermarry with the locals. Perhaps a nonviolent society would need an institution as bloody, dangerous, and ostentatious as bullfighting —a moral substitute for war. (I agree it didn't substitute for the Spanish Civil War.) The last great Roman Emperors—Trajan, Hadrian, Marcus—were colonials from Spain where the old Italian character had emigrated; still today we have there the living picture of the classical world.

The normal act of ancient religion was the sacrifice of a bull on a hot day; his name *Taurus* is shared by most ancient languages. There was some pretense that he walked voluntarily to death. In the human sacrifice of Phoenicia I suppose a semblance of choice was generated by social pressure. Ancient societies were groping to the point when a victim would let himself be sacrificed for the good of something more than a political fatherland. The Real Presence of Jesus in the Eucharist is effected by our solidarity with his revolutionary self-offering. As an oppressed community approaches self-awareness, it makes its own suffering available as an organizing issue around which the oppressed everywhere can build. The violent powerful and the violent powerless are both amnesia victims. By forgetting their own history, they're doomed to repeat it. In what the New Testament calls *anamnesis*, "remembering," the fog of amnesia is dispelled by the fresh wind of *radical nonviolence*.

Probably what Jesus meant was, "Do this [not on some subsequent occasion, but *now*] so that I may be remembered *by God*." The sharing of the group in his self-offering is meant to awake an echo—that is, to be "remembered" in the Structure of being beyond space and time. Since he's a man like us operating in the dark of actual history, his words deal with the concrete present; that's precisely what suited them to serve the future. The reality of his having been remembered by God *then* is insured through his being remembered by us *now*. Memory is an actual prolongation of the past into the present, not through lifeless stones or bones, but through the unbrokenness of living community. The acid of reality in his self-sacrifice dissolved the last remains of his individuality, and liberated him to form the new level of unity in our celebration. His death was identical with his resurrection, he was lifted up in both senses simultaneously. So our joyful victory over death is inseparable from our incorporation into the community of his way.

The waiter at table. As concretely as possible, passing around food and drink to often unappreciative people is meant as training in subordination, a school of nonviolent action. If there are going to be arrests, let it be very clear that the cadre gets busted first. Once that principle is clear, it's widened to insure that *the whole community is the cadre*—each in turn takes the paradoxical leadership position. It intercedes before the Power of history for its own prisoners and casualties, for the needs of other oppressed communities—above all for the powerful, victimized by their inheritance of authority. Our awareness of other people suffering educates us by stirring us to action in the arena of history.

The best service we can offer our brother is transmitting our own motivation and joy. The usual corporal works of mercy are sterile unless they're allowed to bubble up into the biggest one—releasing the body for happiness. Of course there's always the risk that happy people will drink too much or get high or bring down the Man or exploit their buddies. Over against it is the certainty that unhappy people haven't found joy.

The awareness of joy comes and goes, not entirely under our control. We need to rest it on a sureness we know what we're doing. The place where knowledge of the Law and the Prophets existed was the Synagogue— a University and meditation-center all in one. The instructional parts of our freedom meal flow from that root. Without arbitrary imposition of ideas either by individuals or by the group, the form of celebration (older than either) does its own educating. The heart of liberation comes from our study of history, the realization we're not alone. The Establishment Church, to reinforce remembrance of *its* foundations, celebrates the memory of kings, archbishops, persecutors, munificent benefactors. Even so, by popular request it has to include the feast of a Francis beside those of his master. Much more so, the means of instruction in the golden thread of our real history will be a *radical calendar,* commemorating yearly the saints of an authentic humanity.

The community as place of healing. The groups of renewal out across the country and the world, already jelling into some kind of free church movement, are still handcuffed by a guilt for failure. They've claimed to see better and walk more surely than the Establishment churches. Instead they keep lapsing into overt violence, factionalism, compromise like the others. While the chaplains of the white ghetto retire into an alert old age, the champions of the poor fall into nervous breakdown, apostasy, compulsions. Partly it can't be helped and we just stick by them. Partly our solidarity can affirm the community feast as a place of *radical healing*. In that fellowship the community can raise its casualties, heal over factions, bring about reconciliation inside—as a preface to reconciliation of oppressors and oppressed outside. Realistic confession can get the load actually off our back onto the broad shoulders of history. We know the final fall that our periodic lapses into casualty status are pointing ahead to. But if each in turn can be taken up into brotherhood, we have some confidence that the ultimate casualty also is swallowed up into victory.

The normal temptation of a movement for peace or justice is to sacrifice its members, or its cause, or both. The Church is the Movement become conscious of itself. But since it includes in some form all the problems of that world which it belongs to and wants to help, healing begins inside. If its basic concern can be for purity of motives and actions, it's a nucleus of healing, putting behind itself both manipulation of persons in the name of an ideology, and manipulation of truth for alleged human need. It becomes an actual example of what it advocates, a beachhead of the counter-invasion which operates not by force but gentleness.

The Restoration of the Orders

Liturgical forms which put first things first will undercut both the trivial matters where the denominations differ and the basic errors where they're in agreement. By restoring the true history of liberation, in a common meal of pure food and drink, we affirm the unity and renewal of nature and society. The New Covenant of that ancient underground cell of nonviolence becomes the constitution of a global commonwealth.

The sacred calendar celebrates the lifetime of an exemplary man through the yearly agricultural cycle, after the style of the pagan mysteries. But the mysteries were hardly celebrating anything more than that cycle—a god maybe but certainly not a man. A wedding anniversary isn't wholly separate from the wedding; it helps determine retrospectively whether there actually was a wedding in the first place. So the intention of the community to represent the past symbolically makes the past actually present. Our life in community through the liturgy generates whatever will be meaningful in the future. The political prophet sees moving in men's hearts the determinations which one day will produce great events. But we feel working in us the political infrastructure of the universe.

Einstein discovered that in our space-time continuum, by a suitable mathematical transformation, intervals of time can be represented as intervals of space; history is projected onto geometry. The mythical geography of the ancient world spatialized the future—and that more-than-future which has been called eternity. The diamond-sharp outline of the ancient city-state in its geographical setting points to the unity of biology and citizenship. That union is realized in the spiritual geography of the *Revelation* of John—a book which from another viewpoint is a set of rubrics for a community liturgy, threatened and unsubdued by the World Pig from the abyss.

We haven't ever actually been in Eden; the childhood

sexuality to which we attach its mountain-streams looked for it in the future. Solomon and Ezekiel locate it in my own adopted home where the great springs break out from inside Lebanon. Under the Plan Vert, suitable prototype for a World Park, the mountain once again is becoming as Tacitus described it, "among tropic ardors, opaque with shade and confident of snowfalls." Hosea's famous vine of Lebanon, of which we're the branches, grows there in its last refuge from Moslem Puritanism, beside the grain which isn't quickened unless it dies.

From the sacred marriage of the youth and his child bride under their cedar canopy has sprung what George Fox calls a "peaceable people" around the globe, illustrating the sweet reasonableness of reconciliation, each considering his brother above himself. In the restoration of nature, and of our own nature, we've taken out naturalization papers in the city where our true citizenship lies. And when we finally settle down there, what do we find but the secret brook still flowing through its streets, and the golden world-tree of life dropping its purple fruit on the banks? The temple of its civic liturgy, called the "house of the forest of Lebanon," has its pillars of cedar living and branching into a vaulted roof, just as its stones are people. In that virgin woodland of the future with its floor of Solomon's-seal and fern, time and space, nature and history blend into love, and the pillars of Chartres fuse with the sacred grove of Muir Woods; for the forest is the cathedral, and the cathedral is the forest.

Conclusion:
New Containers,
New Contents

It bothers us when somebody hijacks an airliner, because we expect a plane ride to be a place of peace, its only threat airsickness, or thunderheads pushing up from over Chicago, monsoon clouds over Bangkok. The envelope of war and death is only a hundred feet thick. It's easy to see why the upper atmosphere, much more so the moon, should have been thought by early man a place of life. Actually though, as we know, we can only get up there in a simulated city, a crowded tourist-section or space-capsule. We haven't yet left a body on the moon, and all our dead up until now are hidden in the earth or sea—which also, by the same token, hold the secret of life.

The Planet as Our Organizing Base

Whatever exploration or colonization we may now do, Terra is our organizing base. Her body and blood generated the complexities of our biochemistry; and if like the giant Antaeus we get lifted off her for too long, some un-

suspected component of our strength will run thin. Whatever extra-terrestrial societies we enter into treaty with,
the global society of nations is our only proper community. Now that we can move towards the sun, as Milton
predicted, and

> Look downward on that Globe whose hither side
> With light from hence, though but reflected, shines,

the green revolution and the peace revolution are the
most elementary tasks of housekeeping in our forest city.

And those jobs, far beyond our capacity as they seem,
are only the outer consequences of an inner rebuilding.
The New Testament is its definitive statement, called out
by an earlier phase of the ongoing crisis. As we read it, we
can hardly help observing that *its Way is different from
the way of the world.* A wholeness quite other than conventional morality, but still not completely out of sight, is
being laid on us.

The ground swell of political revolution all around
us draws its strength from that same tradition, which it
sees us as inheriting and disowning. If we don't make radical changes along lines that *we* choose, they'll be made for
us along lines that somebody else chooses. We don't let
our kids borrow even nickels from their mothers' pocket-
books, so as not to get into the habit. Much less can we
stand by in silence when somebody cuts down a tree or
starts a war.

A Liberated Church as Our Primary Community

Since the interlocking crisis of violence is unitary, all
of a piece, with damage to nature and society compound-

ing each other, the response has got to be unitary. Any community where that response is made here will have to include a radically liberated Church. Nothing but a crisis of this magnitude could radicalize the existing churches. And even *it* may not, since they, like the other institutions of our society, are in the grip of self-destroying demonic powers. We can just pour out our life and trust to Providence.

We know only too well that we're brothers and sisters of the violent. Every impulse which has led them out of the right course is also working in us. At every turn we have to fall back on the community of love to check us in our tendency to destruction. Our efforts to liberate the churches in conformity with the Gospel are nearly always a failure. But we have to go on because we can't find that community inside the churches as they are. For now that the frontier of exploration is the moon, where no colony of the oppressed can take refuge, world society is the only society we've got. There's no New World left to go and build our sectarian Utopia in.

The weak link in the chain of exploitation is what it was all along intended to be: the Church. Because the United States has a spectrum of denominations with no one dominant, she's more accessible to the message, a potential vanguard of the Gospel. The renewal carried out through Francis was the last one which spent its course fully inside the existing Church. Since then, each century has seen movements for peace and liberation which have gotten cut off from the central tradition of community.

In the *sixteenth* century radical reformers like Menno Simons rediscovered the actual message of Jesus; but they made community into self-contained sects, prone from time to time to lapse into violence.

In the *seventeenth* century George Fox rediscovered the true virtue of peace. But he rejected the symbolic forms of the sacraments by which alone his community would have the power to go on attracting the world to itself. Even so his Friends are the clearest institutional witness to the truth today.

In the *eighteenth* century the Wesleys rediscovered the preaching of Paul, on a deeper level of the psyche than the official Reformation. But they allowed themselves to be pushed out of the existing Church into moralism and anti-intellectualism. Even so they were the driving force behind the Evangelical revival: mission overseas and to the new industrial proletariat, concern for abolition of slavery.

In the *nineteenth* century the cry for liberation was raised among the working poor by Marx, at a time when the evangelical movement was being co-opted by European imperialism into a paternalistic missionary enterprise. But Marxism by its very success has been unable to reach a new subproletariat. Because its secularism cut it off from old symbolism, it attributes to itself a monopoly on justice, ignores its own violence, and assumes its opponents incapable of reason.

In the *twentieth* century out of the soil of Marxism have grown national liberation movements, which moved from secularism to human concern through affirmation of their own cultural roots. With some exceptions they haven't found any alternative to violence—because they didn't see their vanguard role broadly enough. Even so they represent the most hopeful Third Force between the American and Soviet empires.

During these five centuries renewal has been either

divisive, or oriented towards counter-violence, or both. While taking our stand with the renewal movements over against the Establishment, we must alter them in two complementary ways. The threat to the environment forces us to dig ever deeper in eradicating our own tendency to violence, as a prelude to offering nonviolence to our opponent. At the same time we must be clearer than any of our predecessors about our complicity with the exploitative society, and our determination to build a new community *inside it* and not over against it.

The Global Message

We hear rebel messages going out on secret wave-lengths, and we know that action against violence is being taken—hasty and partial, often self-frustrating. How can we reduce the noise-level of the messages? A broadcast bounced off a satellite, simultaneously translated into the principal world languages, overcomes all obstacles to communication but the greatest: distrust of the sender. And we can't wait until some Gandhi or Chavez, at the apex of a pyramid of the disarmed poor, has been able to requisition those channels.

Actually we all know in advance better than any Pope or UN Secretary General how the necessary global message would read. Only we private persons, with no political power, have the freedom of action to build ourselves into voluntary international communities of peace. Standing on that base, we may bypass their monopolistic channels and sent out our own Telstar message, economizing on valuable words:

PEOPLE OF THE WORLD UNITE
WE HAVE NOTHING TO LOSE BUT DISTRUST
OUR BROTHERS ARE GETTING SMASHED
WE ALL HAVE A COMMON INTEREST
OUR SHARED LIFE ON THE PLANET
WE HOLD THAT LIFE IN OUR HANDS
A MAD POWER IS THREATENING IT
WE ARE CALLING A STRIKE FOR IT
THE ENEMY IS NOT PEOPLE
OUR FIDELITY WINS THE DAY

It would be easier to find the right words if we designated beforehand some enemy who didn't have to hear them, and adopted the slogans shared by the other half of humanity. But then our alleged communication would only widen the crack. Standing here in the United States we try just to get an initial hearing from hungry Latin Americans, Asiatics under a police state, detribalized Africans. At the same time we remind our own people that somewhere between Canada and Mexico there may still exist an America on the growing edge of planetary and cosmic history; as yet no Russian or Chinese has stepped into the role of world peacemaker once played by A. J. Muste.

To the Reader

If revolutions are going on, it's because people committed themselves to action before there was any movement to join. If talk about a strike or revolution seems artificial or threatening, I'm glad to drop those metaphors and leave a blank page in the book. The reader may fill it up with what he knows in his heart is the right way for him to be spoken to.

We both are very well aware that things have gone wrong on the globe. And still a power, never yet fully measured, lies in the will of each individual to help set things straight. Ripples of influence join every man and woman to every other. Somebody has calculated that a chain of five personal acquaintances can be built to connect any two individuals in the United States. Since every foreign land has at least one friend in America, we are only a dozen persons away from every soul on the planet. And the planet itself has all along, we now discover, been receiving gravitational waves from the rest of the cosmos, actual deformations of the space-time continuum, as the sleeping galaxies shift in their beds and arouse their neighbors.

The sleepers are rising from the dead—more and more now through our own persistent knocking. The whole universe is illuminated by a cosmic principle which has already found an historic example here: everything can become itself without disturbing its neighbor—in fact to their joint advantage. We're not to underestimate the obstacles in the way of change. Still, independent of our faults, there stand the Saints, objective and free, not without their own blind spots, but mutually correcting each other. And they witness above all that anybody anywhere has the power to throw off the yoke of habit and pass through the waters to the liberation of integrity. Keep in mind, through whatever words are most natural, the changes in society required by the needs of the planet and of the poor; believe that those changes can be made by *your* fidelity and nothing else.

My friend David Nesmith, who saw as much of the war as any American civilian from a farm near Hue, brought back an artillery shell which has been machined into a chalice. It seems to me that this job requires a great deal of pressure, and I don't understand how the Vietnamese do it. Many other things about that remarkable people also escape me. But it's very clear that every other artifact around us, beginning with ourselves, has to undergo just as much reshaping. In this book I've begun to block out concretely what that would involve; if anything I'm sure I've underestimated the difficulty. We will not find our proper environment, sitting down each under his fig tree unafraid, until after the bayonets of the masked battalions have been forged into a plow, and every instrument of our violence has been beaten out into a receptacle for the sap of life.